Muddling T]

Russell Smallwood

Kichaka Publications

Published by Russell Smallwood, Finches, Pembury, Kent TN2 4BA

Printed and bound by
www.impressionit.co.uk

ISBN 0-9547207-0-9

For my family, and remembering those no longer living.

◀ ● ▶

"I think it is terribly important that you keep (revived plays) in period. The relationship between the period as it was when it was lived and the relationship between how one looks at it in hindsight are entirely different."

Stephen Daldry on staging a revival of Priestley's 1945 classic *An Inspector Calls*.

CONTENTS

MAPS

Photographs

CHAPTER ONE

FOR ALMOST seven years from 1924 my parents rented a pretty stone house (a hunting box it would have been called), on Lord Jersey's Oxfordshire estate at Caulcott, five miles north of Bicester. The Great War and an unpleasant stint in Ireland behind them, they were in their mid-thirties, my father a staff captain at the War Office, both were mad keen on hunting. Geraldine, six and a half years older than me, was ten and Antony seven, so a settled home was thought good for us children.

North Oxfordshire was still deep country. A car rarely passed down our village street and as many work horses as hunters came to be shod in the sizzle and reek of the little smithy at Lower Heyford, where I later took my ponies. Three-quarters of a million domestic servants still lived in and much of the pre-1914 social order remained. Farming here had long been in the doldrums. A hunting friend in any of the larger houses in the Bicester country was likely to be a banker, a sugar baron or a brewer, who would emerge from his park gates on non-hunting days to catch the 9.15 up to the City. My father also dashed off to Bicester station most mornings in his red Morgan three-wheeler. But I knew he was in the army because a soldier servant who lived in cleaned the shoes and did the saddlery. Like many girls at the time, Geraldine was not sent away to school until she was thirteen. Meanwhile she and I shared a succession of governesses, who taught me the three R's, and at eight I followed Antony to prep school in Brighton.

My parents were a very sociable couple. My memories of Caulcott are of children's parties, cub-hunting on a leading rein, going to pony club and dancing classes. There were polo matches and tennis parties at Kirtlington Park, children's cricket here and there in the summer. At all of these we would arrive (with luck and almost always late) in Old Henry, the family's large, cumbersome and extremely wayward Angus-Sanderson, 1917 model saloon. At home we had ponies, our bicycles to ride on the empty side roads, there was a grass tennis court, a cinema at Bicester and, perfectly natural at the time, always the freedom to roam. Old army friends of my parents – Monkey Blacker was the Hunt Secretary – lived over at Bucknell, an hour away across country by pony. Later, aged nine, when Olive schooled me and my pony for the Bicester horse show, nobody questioned my riding back and forth through the woods and fields alone.

Both of my parents had been only children. Our grandmother Didi (rhymed with 'hifi') who helped me greatly through life by teaching me to do my multiplication tables 'dodging', as she called it, was sadly our only real grandparent. When her husband, Charles Wade, a partner in the eponymous family firm of steel stockholders in Birmingham, died while still in his forties in 1907, Didi and their only child, my mother Beatrice, stayed on at Sandal House, Solihull, where we children were later born.

Financially as well as emotionally it was my father who had drawn the short straw. Sadly his mother died having him, her first child, in 1889. His father, also Charles, then married again, had five more children and himself died only a year after Charles Wade. Not taking to his stepmother, my father had remained at Rigby Hall in Bromsgrove with his grandfather, Robert, a prosperous JP who ran the family's wine business set up in Birmingham a hundred and fifty years earlier.

Just nineteen when his father left him with the crippling burden of five children to be educated, my father never mentioned his half-siblings again. After a brief spell in the family wine business he secured a commission, rather late, through the army's Supplementary Reserve. The two families already knew one another, and when in 1913 my parents married, Didi was able to make her daughter a handsome allowance of £500 a year – as much as a teacher earned and almost three times a subaltern's pay. Though badly hit later in the 1929 crash, it was at this time largely Didi's financial support that made their lifestyle possible.

A lonely child, my father had been brought up by an adoring maiden aunt, Gertrude, last daughter but one amongst Robert's nine children, whom we children would call 'Granny'. Granny Gertrude, a confirmed Londoner whom we saw frequently and loved dearly, had two sisters, great-aunts Maggie and Estelle, probably then in their early sixties and very well disposed. Unfortunately they appeared on my horizon much less often, invariably in tandem, both always dressed in black or dark blue and, to me, similarly old. It was Estelle, the sharper and actually six years the younger, who first said one day "You don't know which I am, now do you, Russell?" As often as not I guessed wrong. It was of course my poor mother who got the blame.

I was still at prep school when our roots were wrenched from the Oxfordshire countryside. Posted briefly to command the East

Yorkshire regimental depot in Beverley, my father went on to instruct gentleman cadets, as they were called, at the R.M.C., Sandhurst, and two years later became a brigade major at the Duke of York's headquarters in London.

By chance a very rich acquaintance of my parents was about to leave for Cairo, where he would spend a couple of years as an honorary attaché at our embassy, and he offered my parents the use of his London home for only the cost of the rates. No. 7 Cheyne Walk was a tall, elegant, beautifully furnished building at an exceptionally prestigious address. Aged 11 I was soon being squashed by my mother for showing off 'our' grand new home to a school friend. The large library, the room we used most, looked out over a substantial garden from the first floor. Decorated by the owner's artistic wife to simulate being under the surface of a pond, the walls and a huge carpet were in shades of green and the ceiling painted in pond-weed swirls of green and yellow. I thought it amazing and rather nice. One door led into an even larger, formal black and white drawing room with a grand piano that looked out across a private road and gardens to the Embankment and the handsome Albert Bridge. Through the other door on the landing was a marvellous speaking tube; pull out the plug and blow – a whistle would sound for the servants down in the basement. Random whistling was banned because it pestered the cook, but I could natter endlessly down it to friends on different floors. There were back stairs with access, I think, to all of the six floors as well as a main staircase, which created endless possibilities for games of 'Murder'.

From Cheyne Walk my father could walk to the Duke of York's headquarters, where we children had the use of the tennis courts. From there I would sometimes slip away into the King's Road to pore over the many jewellers' showcases and perhaps trade one of my half-hunter watches, bought for about £1 each and gold at least in colour. (Half-hunters must have been deeply unfashionable.) Curiosity satisfied, I could drift home down Flood Street. Nobody in those days thought anything would happen to a small boy.

Our new green Rover saloon, smaller than Old Henry, had a curious canvas-like body you could press in with a finger. After a memorable holiday in South Mull, when my father was at risk of overstaying his leave, she brought home the five of us, plus Shrimp, the Cairn terrier, a cat in a basket and a mountain of luggage, four hundred miles from the mean cobbled streets of Paisley in one blessedly sleep-strewn session. Mostly she sat quietly outside our house, looking fittingly modest between two Rolls-Royces. 'Daring raid on Major's home' I remember the evening paper said when we were burgled during dinner. The house was in fact entered three times during those two years, and whatever jewellery my parents owned was stolen.

My second prep school, Langley Place, St Leonards, having got me through the common entrance, I was supposed to be cushioned on entering Wellington College by the presence in the Picton dormitory of Antony. Wellington in the thirties was going through a bad patch, I have been told, bumping along on the auto-pilot of custom while an elderly Master, F.B. Malim, stayed too long in his post. All male and pretty philistine, with a constant under-swell of sex, we lived by numerous rules and customs concerning fagging, who was senior enough to do this or that, what games to watch, free time, bounds. Conform or transgress at the risk of being beaten, as I was quite often. Patriotism was certainly encouraged and I think we were all rightly proud of the large areas then coloured red on the school atlases. We poured into chapel and swung out again in military fashion, heels rattling on the gratings beside the Master's stall, fourteen times each week. Dutifully we cheered at the end of school matches we had barely noticed, played the fool in the art class (even if, like me, you rather enjoyed it) and in general tried to escape the eye of authority.

Malplaquet House, Malplaquet Barracks, Marlborough Lines – an address that could only be in Aldershot. From the public road below the C.O.'s four-square brick house a series of single-storey buildings lined identical macadam side-streets, a large open space at one end was the battalion parade ground. Soldiers marched about in serge and heavy boots with puttees neatly wound, stamped to attention as an officer passed. Away to the right were Oudenarde Barracks and Ramillies, Marlborough's identical trio, which made up the brigade.

For the first time I was seeing ordinary regimental army life, my father commanding what we always called from the military signposts '2E York R', the Second Battalion of the East Yorkshire Regiment. In 1935 the regiment had just celebrated its 250th anniversary with a visit of inspection from the Duke of York, later King George VI, which was deemed a great success notwithstanding my deep embarrassment at the art deco brass buckle that slanted across my mother's skull-fitting new hat. The occupant of Malplaquet House was enjoying his powers, as much kingpin of his domain as the captain of any ship. His regimental riding team had achieved the impossible by beating a much richer cavalry regiment at the Aldershot Show, my father himself winning

6

the highly competitive class for officers' chargers. As he would maintain afterwards, commanding 2E York R was the most enjoyable period of his career.

Holidays in Aldershot were fun. Alternating with thrilling duels between Sapper's Bulldog Drummond and the evil Petersens, there was plenty of tennis and squash at the club, occasional golf with Antony, riding lessons on the RMC's horses at Sandhurst and the chance to hire one for hunting. While my mother busied herself with the married quarters, Geraldine found time from the subalterns' attentions to run a large pack of cub scouts. The boys were the sons of 'other ranks' in the regiment, together with a sprinkling of townsfolk, and I joined them once for their annual camp. At home no one talked politics and in the absence of TV I had seen virtually nothing of the way of life of anyone who did not live with servants in much the way we did. I realised of course that it was not right for Wellington's Walworth Mission boys to look so raggedly poor, and it seemed unfair that so few of Geraldine's cubs had ever seen the sea. Wondering vaguely what would it be like if one were not privileged, I remember thinking with all the egotism of youth that if people from any background *could* get into a public school, or go on to Oxford, or be accepted at Sandhurst for a commission, the competition would be simply awful. One should not say so, but perhaps it was just as well they couldn't. This, I confess, was about all I had at the time of social conscience.

Leaving late after packing up the cub camp we stopped our car half off the road deep in the New Forest to eat our sandwiches. At the end of a long straight stretch I noticed a speck appear, a distant van speeding towards us. Then there was a roar, a bang and a tinkle. Life might have ended right there: the driver had passed so close that he knocked off our hubcap.

The end of the next summer holiday found me for some reason in quarantine, healthy and at home. Saying in typical fashion that I needed proper exercise, my father suggested I put on Wellington Officers' Training Corps uniform and join his 'A' Company for a route march. Agreement being expected, when a grinning column of soldiers halted early next morning in front of our house, I gave the Colonel a shambling salute and fell myself in. The company commander, a major hardened by many seasons of hot marches on the northwest frontier, mercifully let me off with a modest fifteen miles. Faute de mieux, it seemed from then on I was destined for the army.

That year Antony left Wellington, going first to learn German in Munich, then to a family in France, and aged fifteen I was formally beaten for 'not working'. Was this the college's final admission of a total failure to help me enjoy learning? At the parental conference that followed the Christmas term report, my father came up with what seemed an ideal solution. "You can pass your school certificate this coming year if you put your mind to it" he informed me. "When you have, you can leave – and you can go on to Munich."

When George V lay dying, the radio fatuously assured us his last words had been "How is the Empire?" "Bugger Bognor" appealed to us much better. Chosen with Eton's OTC to line the funeral route near St George's Chapel, Windsor, we were quickly practised in inverting the 'present arms' to rest the rifle muzzles on our toes, 'arms reversed'. At Windsor the bier and its cortege moved slowly past. Swivelling my right eyeball I caught a glimpse of our new King Edward VIII, wearing a remarkably long grey overcoat and looking like everyone else, glum. After that I suspect we all peeked a little to watch the passing of the largest collection of crowned heads we should see in our lifetimes. Edward's behaviour and the Second World War would soon sweep away, not only most of the Kings themselves, but the remnants of that almost mystical reverence for our monarchy which was felt throughout their lives by my parents and many of their generation, but not by mine.

Returning in the summer of 1936 to the Chateau de Castellier in Normandy following a visit the previous year with my mother, I took my cherished bicycle with me, and after a fortnight with the family, whose fine house would suffer a direct hit during the Normandy invasion, I set off from Lisieux towards Brittany. Sadly, little memory remains of those peaceful fifty mile a day rides – of quiet pedalling along empty sunlit roads, rarely a car to be seen. After a few nights in small auberges, a telegram at the pre-arranged hotel in Dinard told me that my father and 2E York R had been ordered immediately to Palestine. Secretly pleased to be spared the loneliness of a long ride across to Le Havre, I put my bike on a train and hurried home.

With my school certificate narrowly secured, I was free to leave at Christmas. The big, indeed the only news that last term, was of the King and Mrs Wallis Simpson. Crowding again into Mr & Mrs Scott's drawing room, we crouched in our dressing gowns to hear Edward's abdication speech, his betrayal of a trust. No one had much to say afterwards. As my father had already left for Palestine, my mother arrived alone to say an awkward goodbye to their friends the Scotts, who thought my departure premature. I would never pass into Sandhurst now: it was all a huge mistake .... loading my school trunk into the boot, we slipped unobtrusively down the back drive.

Antony had probably been reticent. Certainly I embarked on the long train journey down to Munich quite unconscious what to expect. There it was a Sunday afternoon early in January 1937, snow on the ground. Plump, friendly Marie Rose, the Stengel's eighteen year old daughter who met me with a car at the Hauptbahnhof had, it seemed, taken a shine to nineteen-year-old Antony and his attractive smile. She explained in quite good English that there were two other English students already in residence: as both were several years older than me I had been allocated a small bedroom on the top floor.

At number 5, Hess Strasse, a substantial three-storey town house in a good residential street, a maid helped me with my luggage and led me across the carpeted hall into a stiffly furnished drawing room. The baroness, a thickset lady around fifty, no doubt concluded on the spot that I was much too young for her ménage. After introducing me to her husband, who was kindly, considerably older and did not much concern himself with the young PG's, she began straight away to lay down the house rules. Be punctual for all meals, no English to be spoken to the other guests. I would not for the present be allowed out after dark. My lessons would start next day, she said. As the teacher lived near enough, I could return for lunch.

Somewhat chastened, I was escorted next morning by Marie Rose to a flat some ten minutes walk away in the Franz Joseph Strasse. There my new teacher, a Dr Anton Pfeiffer, proved to be a shortish man in his forties with dark already thinning hair, a pince-nez and an enormous balloon of a stomach. He spoke some English although not fluently. Most intriguing I found, was the way in which, fingers interlocked below his vast paunch, he would occasionally hoick it up with the inside of his forearms. It was a gesture that I came later to watch for. An experienced schoolmaster with two boys of his own, he soon put me at ease.

Meals in the Hess Strasse were formal and served by parlour maids. Although the other students could usually contribute something, I had only scraped a German pass in the school certificate and found myself confined to 'butter, bitte' or sometimes a mumbled three word answer to a direct question. Back from lessons around tea time I would do my homework, then read or hang around until dinner. From 9.00 pm onwards several times a week, the doorbell would ring and a succession of the Stengels' middle-aged friends and neighbours would be formally announced. Baron this, baroness that – everyone in the German fashion had a title of some sort. Their coats removed, guests made for the drawing room where, seated around the room on formal chairs, they made polite conversation while the Frau Baronin, assisted by Marie Rose, poured cups of tea from a large silver teapot and a maid handed around cakes.

After that it was our turn. Any house guest not out for dinner, and I was the only one obliged *always* to stay in, had to be introduced to each visitor in turn. The Baroness, being a deeply committed snob, usually started my introduction with a paean about Lord Haig, the young English earl with a household name, who had been my immediate (and far more worthy) predecessor. "Dear D.....", she would say while introducing me, "such a shame he had to leave us. Of course he will have had his responsibilities back in Scotland. But so easy in the house, and his German coming along so well.... this is Russell."

The ordeal of well-intentioned questions and the mortifying struggle for words that followed could only be evaded on the plea of additional homework, which I soon began to invent. Forbidden to talk English downstairs, I started to invade the older boys' room, either to complain about the Baroness or simply to chatter. No doubt I disturbed their work and was a pain. Marie Rose told me how much better Antony had behaved, and how much harder he had worked; of course that did not help either.

Matters came to a head after about six weeks. Finally I was to be allowed out with one of the other boys, presumably to celebrate my seventeenth birthday. My nineteen year old companion met up with older friends. Someone had a car, we moved from one beer cellar to the next. By 2.00am I had drunk, or later claimed to have drunk, the equivalent of a gallon. Back at Number 5 they helped me to the bottom of the staircase where, caught by a sudden retch, I brought up most of it on the Stengels' hall carpet. Later, clutching at my heaving, gyrating bed, falling off, scrambling back, I swore I would never again get paralytically drunk. A promise I have kept.

Predictably the row next morning was final. Under pressure from Marie Rose, the Baroness at length conceded I would have to stay on until my parents, now both in Egypt where my father had a new job, could make other arrangements. She would write to them at once. Meanwhile I was not to go out or to talk to the other guests: I was to be put firmly in Coventry.

That morning I arrived very late at the Franz Joseph Strasse, hung over and distinctly scared. Herr Pfeiffer opened the door. He listened briefly to my story, then asked his plump, motherly wife, who was hovering uncomprehendingly in the background, to bring me a prairie oyster. Once I had swallowed it and been sent to lie down for half an hour he sat me at the table. "It is quite clear" he pronounced, "that you can't stay on at Baron Stengel's. Why not come and live here? There is a room – the boys can double up. I will write to your father."

Before dark I collected a few things from the Hess Strasse and spoke briefly to Marie Rose. Clearly relieved, she said my trunk would be sent on, I need not see the Baroness again. That episode, thank goodness, was over.

CHAPTER TWO

NEXT MORNING the shops began to open opposite my second floor window on the Franz Joseph Strasse. People emerged from the doorways of other apartments like ours, picking their way to work through the pavement slush, or crunching across a wide expanse of snow-covered cobbles as yet unmarked by car tracks. From my left came the grind and squeal of metal wheels, and now and then the clang of a tram's bell in the Elizabethan Platz, where Dr Pfeiffer taught at a large state school. Last for breakfast, I would eat alone at the communal table in the flat's central living room. Afterwards I worked there with Dr Pfeiffer until 12.30 pm and later with his taller, more reticent brother, also a teacher, during the afternoon. When Peter (aged 15) and Rudi (aged 12) came in for lunch my books would be removed, Frau Pfeiffer would cover the red chenille tablecloth with a white one and set down a tureen of hot soup. After grace had been said, Dr Pfeiffer would take up the large table napkin beside him, tuck a corner of it into his collar and spread the remainder carefully across his ample circumference. Then, telling the boys to talk clearly, he would reach for the ladle.

The world, and particularly the Baroness, would have seen my translation to the Pfeiffers – five people in a three-bedroomed flat with only a part-time maid servant – as a plunge down the social snake. No doubt it was. However, I was soon happy there and awaited my father's reply to my letter with some trepidation. When it came, to my surprise, he seemed entirely unconcerned about my shameful conduct at the Stengels. Asking only whether I really wanted to live with the Pfeiffers, he said if I did, he would send a monthly draft. This would cover my board and tuition and should be handed over immediately. In a departure from former practice (the Stengels had doled out my pocket money) he would add twenty marks (then £1) per week as spending money. My board, lodging and £1 per week! What munificence!

"Hire a bike", the Pfeiffers advised. I did so and found my life transformed. The only English (or in his case, Irish) paying guest nearby was Terence Prittie (later Lord Dunsany), whom I met again a decade later, when he was for many years correspondent in Germany for the Manchester Guardian. Although an amusing, far more mature twenty, Terence seemed glad enough to have my company for skiing trips. Most weekends that winter we would meet around 5.30 am at the Starnbergerbahnhof and take a third class, wooden bench return to Mittenwald. Ski lifts were still unknown and at fashionable Garmisch Partenkirchen, which boasted the only funicular operating in the Bavarian Alps, it would have cost my whole allowance to go up the Zugspitze. Having hired skis for me (Terence had his own) we would choose our day's run. Traversing across the steeper slopes, buckskins on if it was too icy, we began to climb, pausing occasionally to puff, to admire the view, or both. By 9.30 am we were usually up at the ski hut, more than ready for our packed breakfasts and a glass or two of gluhwein with other skiers by the fire. After that it was climb up, ski down until afternoon.

When it was time to go Terence, much the stronger skier, pushed off first. "See you at the station". Twenty minutes later, crashing for the third time near the tree line, I brushed off the snow and looked around. Not a soul in sight. It is cold without a glove, my buttons stubborn, but at last a luxurious arching stream sizzles yellow holes and patterns into the soft virgin snow. "How many falls this time?" Terence asks as we wait for our train. "Two", I lie, "and I stopped for a pee". Back in Munich before dusk, the damage, including ski hire, would never exceed ten shillings.

Grand opera was performed in the elegant setting of the National Theatre on the Maximilian Platz, sadly destroyed in the war. Seats up in the amphitheatre cost about three marks and were, even to me, amazingly cheap. International singers like Ranczek kept the standard high and my tiny allowance took me on fortnightly visits to some twenty different operas.

As spring advanced news came that my family were to assemble en masse in Bavaria. My father, now a full Colonel and stationed in Cairo, was coming with my mother and Geraldine overland by car from Venice; Antony would bring out the two grannies by train from London. Although happy for me Dr Pfeiffer began to fidget like a bride's mother. Would the Colonel approve of this or that? Was I really satisfied with my room? It was not simply a worry about money that made him nervous (hard up though the Pfeiffers undoubtedly were) or because I was the first PG they had taken in (and might conceivably lose). Inherently I think Dr Pfeiffer, like many middle-aged, middle class Germans at the time, regarded Britain and her empire, and the status the English then enjoyed in Europe, with considerable awe. Although no snob he would talk respectfully of the 'English chentleman'. My father, an English Colonel, was a person of some consequence whose good opinion he genuinely coveted.

In the event, my parents' call on the Pfeiffers proved friendly but short – all smiles and handshakes, mainly because none on the distaff side had a word of language in common. Afterwards we went on a tour of Munich, which ended at one of the long wooden tables in the Hofbraeuhaus, Munich's largest and most famous bierkeller. A beefy female arrived to take our order, three steins foaming in each massive fist. My mother said she would prefer a cup of tea.

Antony and the older generation arrived next day. All of us then moved on in the surprising opulence of my parents' large new Lincoln Zephyr to a hotel in Berchtesgaden (where we did not, of course, see either Hitler or his mountain retreat), then to the summer music festival at Salzburg, whence the grannies returned to England. Staying as paying guests at the Burghof Allentsteig near the Czech border for some partridge shooting, my father suddenly announced he would like to test my German. Knowing he had passed the army interpretership, and considerably in awe of my quick-witted and physically imposing parent (even when rebellious), I wanted to do both myself and Dr Pfeiffer justice. After the viva-voce had gone well he handed me a piece of prose. Haltingly, I struggled through the usual convolutions of a German text. It was about a butcher. *"Er erwischte den Schweiss von der Stirn...."* he wiped the sweat from his brow. I had not a clue what the words meant. What might a village butcher conceivably be doing? "He separated the fat from the lean," I pronounced confidently and my father laughed until he gasped. In the outcome, patient Dr Pfeiffer and I were both reckoned to have passed.

While Antony stayed in Linz to fish, Geraldine and I hired a two-man canoe and for two glorious sunlit days slid peacefully down the Danube, paddling where the great river was wide and slow, steering only as strong currents swept us through narrows and around bends. I remember little traffic. Nearing Vienna, a steamer stopped at our second riverside inn, took the canoe on board and returned us to Linz, more noisily, but in hours. Reunited with my parents, we visited the ancient Benedictine Abbey at Melk, admired the Lipizaner white horses at practice in Vienna and drove on to Budapest. As Antony returned home and I to Munich the others turned south to catch a boat at Dubrovnik.

An Anglo-Egyptian treaty had been signed the previous year resulting in the appointment of a British Military Mission to train the Egyptian army. My father, was now Chief of Staff to Major-General Marshall-Cornwall (later General Sir James). Like everyone else on the staff he had diplomatic status, hence the smug CD plates on our tax-free new car, and he was paid by the Egyptian government rather than the War Office. "Between entre nous", my mother confided (one of her better malapropisms) "he is getting £2,000 a year – tax free!" It was this largesse that had made the whole trip possible.

The temperature rose into the nineties. With all the schools in Munich closed, Peter, Rudi and I lay around the pool in the Englischer Garten, played handball with their older cousins or sucked on the little water ices sold from kiosks all over the city. At only ten pfennigs each I became quite addicted; seventeen in a morning could have been a local record!

As my German began to improve I often biked into the city centre, watching from the back of a huge Nazi rally on the

Maximillian Platz, or mingling with the enthusiastic crowds when Hitler and his motorcade drove in procession with Mussolini to the Rathaus. A pair of smartly uniformed SS men were always posted in front of the Feldherrnhalle. It was in a street to their right, the Residenz Strasse, that Hitler's first bid for power had failed. As the Baedeker of the time noted, there was 'a memorial to the sixteen National Socialists who fell in the fighting of 9 November 1923; passers by salute with the 'Deutscher Gruss' (right arm extended)'. The ploy here was to walk nonchalantly past the guards, without of course extending the right arm. One could shift one's bike or books quickly from the left hand into the right, or look suddenly the other way – always getting an exciting frisson. Whether it was really a part of the guards' function to stop anyone who did not salute I have no idea; I never saw this happen.

One evening in the opera foyer, the crowd suddenly parted. Into the hush came the Führer himself dressed in the brown shirt of SA uniform and followed by his entourage. Smiling, and more burly than I expected, he passed close by and up the stairs. It was the only time I saw him at such close quarters. As I soon found out, everyone was cautious in talking about the government. The Stengels and their friends never directly criticised the party but left the impression they found the National Socialists socially not quite 'people like us.' Whatever they might be getting up to, it was better not to talk about it. The elderly Graf and Graefin Pappenheim, with whom Terence lived in their smallish flat, would sometimes invite me to splendidly Edwardian teas where the table was always heaped with good silver. Both the Hauptgraf and his wife, impoverished descendants of an imperial general of the Thirty Years War and one of the great families of Austro-Hungarian nobility, spoke excellent English and were invariably kind to me. They liked to talk about anything and everywhere, but usually in the past, so what they thought about Hitler (if they brought themselves to think about him at all) remained a closed book.

As time went on, Dr Pfeiffer began here and there to reveal himself. During the 1920's he had been a member of the Bavarian Diet and had even held a minor post in the state government. When the Weimar Constitution was annulled by Hitler and the Diet abolished his post disappeared and he had been forced to return to teaching. Much worse, as a former political opponent he had been interviewed by the Gestapo and blacklisted. Now he knew he would never get promotion. Like every German I met that year, Dr. Pfeiffer agreed with Hitler about one thing – the Treaty of Versailles had been unreasonably harsh and unfair to Germany. For that reason the doctor had gone along willingly with the reoccupation of the Rhineland the previous year and been glad of the upsurge in national pride that resulted. "But it isn't going to stop there" he would proclaim gloomily, hitching up his stomach "sooner or later Hitler will go too far. He is bound to have a war .... *muss einen Krieg haben.* England will come in, then America. We shall lose again and Germany will be totally destroyed". *"Denkst du denn, Anton?"* his cosy, domesticated wife would interpose anxiously, but the boys usually stayed silent. Another source of anxiety, about which the doctor spoke openly on several occasions, was the concentration camps, nearby Dachau in particular. Acquaintances from his own political past had been sent there and had not returned. "Many Jews get taken" he told me, "and there are beatings – they get terrible treatment".

I sometimes wondered what blond, solid Peter made of these

near-subversive remarks. Rudi, who was a bubbly, cheeky boy, may have thought little of it, but at fifteen Peter must have had an opinion. Whatever they thought, neither boy ever discussed the regime with me or talked about the future. Once a week they would dress in their Hitler Jugend uniforms and dash out, apparently willing and cheerful, to a Nazi meeting. Children of their time.

Not much older than the Pfeiffer boys myself, I was by no means uninfluenced by the propaganda I read in the newspapers and the widespread enthusiasm for Hitler's new Germany, regularly evident on the streets. In the autumn of 1937 a large, well advertised art exhibition was being shown at the Deutsches Museum on a small island in the Isar, *Entartete Kunst* (Degenerate Art). It sounded rather intriguing and one afternoon I rode down on my bike to have a look. Inside the gallery only an occasional murmur could be heard from the sizeable crowd. Some of the oil paintings around the walls were distorted and abstract, the kind of unintelligible modern work Hitler was known to dislike, others were representational. Under each was a typewritten official commentary.

Most of these paintings, I gradually realised, were supposed either to have been painted by, or to feature, Jews. Their topics were often crude to the point of disgusting. In one, stirring still fresh memories of the hyper-inflation of 1923, Jewish profiteers with whorls of greasy, dangling locks and hooked noses leered from behind their moneybags at starving women and children begging for alms. In a second, blood dripped from fingers and splashed the overalls of kosher butchers in a blood-soaked slaughterhouse. Another showed freemasons up to no good in sinister, secret conclave. The propaganda was completely blatant, yet the sheer quantity of pictures, and particularly those pseudo-sociological 'explanations' under each began to make me feel extremely uncomfortable. Did the Nazis have a point? I knew very little about Jews. In England they were often the butt of family jokes. Rated mercenary and flashy – the 'Yid's Bentley' they called the new Jaguar – most people blamed them for our current troubles in Palestine. Everyone at this state-sponsored exhibition, I began to notice, was looking extremely serious. I could see my face reflected in the glass of the pictures. My hair appeared pitch black, nose decidedly prominent. What if someone, or the exhibition authorities, thought I might be Jewish? Alarm bells began to ring. Shaming though it is to admit, I was thoroughly relieved to slip out through the doors.

Soon after this my father wrote to Dr Pfeiffer saying I needed coaching for the army exam in other subjects and he would like to have me in Cairo by Christmas. "So lovely to have you at home, darling" my mother wrote, "besides, everyone here speaks French, so it will be just as good for you as going to France."

Travelling by train and boat from Venice, I was met at Port Said and installed next to Geraldine in my parents' Cairene flat on Gezira, a large island in the middle of the Nile. Light and airy, although not in those days air-conditioned (wet blankets were hung over the doorways in hot weather), their flat was in a tree-lined avenue only a quarter of a mile from the fashionable Gezira sporting club. Here, as in every dependent territory, the better-off English met to exercise, to eat or just to gossip around the pool. All around the Eastern Mediterranean, in Egypt as in Greece, the educated communicated in French. This was therefore to be my focal subject and my parents had booked me lessons with a much recommended Syrian. As for other subjects on the Sandhurst syllabus, a crammer would try to bring me up to scratch in history (1789 – 1914), what passed then for geography, and maths. Meanwhile it was the holidays – so have fun!

After 350 years under the Turks, and occupied since 1872 by the British, Egypt had recently become, nominally at least, independent. Whatever the Treaty might say, with British troops guarding the canal, units of the fleet in Alexandria and at Suez, a cavalry regiment and several battalions of infantry stationed in the citadel and around Cairo, she still looked and felt very much like a part of the empire. At the pinnacle of British influence and doyen of the foreign community stood our ambassador, Sir Miles Lampson (later Lord Killearn), who had until recently been styled High Commissioner for Egypt and the Sudan. Very grand and imperial he was still, and was said to have the young King Farouk in his pocket. Although the British Overseas Airways Corporation had just begun regular flights to India, the vast majority of passengers travelled to and fro by boat and maidens of the 'fishing fleet' en route there for a husband would stop off to land a catch in Egypt – such at any rate was the local cliché.

In size, if not in social prestige, the British Military Mission ranked almost with our embassy. Marshall-Cornwall, the locally titled General Pasha whom my father, the Colonel Bey, now served was reckoned very clever and held army interpreterships in eleven languages. No one, however, much envied his task, which was to create an effective Egyptian army. The Egyptian soldier was reckoned good material but their officers mostly fat and hopeless. Indeed rumour had it that promotion to the rank of major and above was made solely on the basis of weight.

Before leaving Munich I had cut a longish article out of the *Frankfurter Zeitung*. Translating this over Christmas, I thought the views it expressed on such matters as Germany's right to the return of her colonies and her need for more *Lebensraum* were probably insufficiently appreciated outside Germany: by an article based on it I might enlighten people and in the process earn myself some useful cash. Rather pleased with the result, I gave it to my father to read. Next morning, looking unusually serious, he called me into his study. Why, he wanted to know, did I think it right to spread pro-Nazi and anti-British propaganda? Receiving no reply, he began to speak warmly and at some length about Britain's achievements and her probity. I listened flabbergasted. While like most boys I admired my father, I thought him on an entirely different plane. Finding that he really minded what I wrote I was touched and probably grew up a little. The article and its Nazi influences went into the bin.

Life at the Pfeiffers had been pleasant but sometimes a bit drab; lessons over, a spurt of ragging with the Pfeiffer boys could be about all there was to do. Here in Cairo, where the sun shone every day, I could ride with Geraldine in the grounds of the Gezira Club. The stately Mohammed in his long white kanzu served lunch, bare feet slapping gently on the polished parquet floor. In the afternoon there might be regimental polo, the celebrated von Cramm could be playing tennis at the club, or I could simply improve my tan by the pool.

As I neared eighteen, Geraldine took me one day in the big Lincoln to the outer limits of Heliopolis and turned off the tarmac. Ahead lay a dead flat, shale littered pan of hard sand which stretched to the horizon. "Feel safe enough?" she asked. "It's a hundred and fifty miles to Suez". With space like this and no driving test to pass it did not take long to get a licence. At Easter Cairo grew uncomfortably hot. Obligingly my sister had me along to camp and swim with some of her subaltern friends way down on the Gulf of Suez. Returning in the torrid heat of afternoon, the sticky tarmac on a ruler-straight embankment across the desert kept dissolving into trembling lakes of mirage. Over the roar of Geraldine's small Ford engine we began to notice a little clickety-click, which increased gradually to knock-knock. After two hours wait by the dead flat Suez-Cairo road, not even a pi dog had come along. To an intrusive thump-thump from the big end we could only drive slowly on. Dusk fell. Of course finally a lorry did take us in tow; but the engine was a write-off.

Working quite hard with my tutors, and anyway too young for the endless round of Gezira drinks parties, I seldom came in for the ubiquitous champagne cocktail, which cost the diplomatic community only five shillings (25p) a bottle. Every sensible host's first choice, it was usually served in pretty stemless glasses, hand-blown in various colours and incorporating bubbles. They were sold in the Muski for eight to the shilling.

The entrance exam for Sandhurst being held in London in June 1938, I was to stop off with the Pfeiffers en route to brush up my German. Waiting at Cairo station for the train to start I dashed off at the last moment to the bookstall. Stretching out for a magazine I had my wallet beside me, which instantly disappeared with everything – journey money, boat and train tickets, and my passport. Luckily my father's diplomatic status helped. When we sailed via a stop at Rhodes into the Piraeus I found money awaiting me. We passed through the Corinth Canal and at the consulate in Trieste, hey presto! another passport.

It was an interesting time to be back in Munich. Weeks earlier Hitler had invaded and occupied, or as most of the British press put it, 'raped' little Austria. No German I met saw it as rape or even occupation, saying truthfully that the cameras proved a large proportion of the population had welcomed their troops. They preferred to call it *Anschluss* – two German-speaking countries combining.

At the Pfeiffers that May I was as much guest as pupil. The *Anchluss* had been highly popular; even the doctor, always fearful of what Hitler would do next, did not condemn it. Everywhere the mood was much more nationalistic, party supporters more assertive than before. Sometimes in a bierkeller a group of youths would come over, trying to goad us into saying something critical of the Führer. The atmosphere could quickly turn nasty. I have often wondered since, not only about the Pfeiffer boys, but whether Dr Pfeiffer himself continued to stick to his guns. As one success followed another over the next three years, did his conviction that Hitler was malign and his war would spell disaster ever waver? I hope not, though it can have done him no good.

Antony, now training with Morgan Grenfell to become a stockbroker, was living with Didi at Chatsworth Court, a modern block of flats in W8. Joining him there I sat the army exam and went before a selection board. In August my parents and Geraldine met us on the north Sutherland coast, where a covey or two of canny grouse lurked on the hotel moor, for our last family holiday. My exam results came through: thanks to languages I had passed in eighth. Higher than expected, this warranted a prize cadetship.

Wellington had been so sure that if I left early I would fail altogether; now it seemed from the published list that no-one from the college's Army VI form had achieved the top ten. I was chuffed, my father quietly delighted.

Officers at this time were trained either at the Royal Military College, Sandhurst or the Royal Military Academy at Woolwich, applicants for cavalry or infantry commissions going to the RMC, while Woolwich catered for the higher technical demands of budding gunners (RA) and sappers (RE). At Sandhurst the elegant 'Old Building' dating from the end of the 18th century, had a wide stone perron leading to an imposing central portico and housed two companies of 'GC's' as we were invariably known. A larger E-shaped, two-storey edifice from 1911, imaginatively entitled 'New Building', held another three companies. The total complement of the college was 600 cadets.

Posted to Number 1 Company in the New Building, I found myself in a platoon commanded by Lieutenant Bernard Fergusson. An Old Etonian, later to become famous as a leader of Wingate's Chindits in Burma, he was a tall, elegant figure who combined the regimental kilt of the Black Watch with the use of a monocle – Lord Peter Wimsey recast by Buchan. By coincidence he had been at the RMC himself seven years earlier in the company commanded by my father.

For the first fourteen weeks of our junior term GCs were 'on the square'. Day after day a team of drill sergeants from the Brigade of Guards worked up our standard of foot and arms drill virtually to that of the foot guards. Under the legendary RSM Brittain, their bellowed and often highly personal admonitions were clearly audible at a hundred paces, always concluding with the obligatory "Mr So-and-So, *Sir!*" Dismissed from parade we had five minutes ("at the double now") to fall in again, impeccably redressed in red-and-white striped blazers and pillbox hats for PT, or in riding kit, and be marched off to the next session. Usually exhausted by the evening, we retired to cubicles little bigger than those at Wellington, to polish boots, brasso buttons and clean our .303 rifles for the next inspection.

Although Sandhurst was in many respects an extension of boarding school, games were not compulsory. Having not volunteered for rugby that autumn, I was playing only squash when one evening a senior knocked on my door and asked if I would like to enter for the juniors' inter-company boxing. My experience of boxing at Wellington had begun and ended (very willingly) at thirteen – however I thought I knew about this. "Everyone enters" my father had assured me from his time at the college "unless they are wet. It's expected". So I put down my name.

Over the next few days I was somewhat alarmed to find that no-one else I knew had entered for the competition, which would take the form of a three-round knockout – in my case, I thought, all too probably. On the dreaded day, my opponent, who had boxed for his public school and must have expected someone of equal calibre, spent the whole of the first round circling, poking cautiously at my prudently high guard. Some time in the next round, urged on by my second to "open up" I rushed in, flailing my arms, whereupon he finally saw the light, and throughout the last punched me purposefully around the ring. "Good bout" Bernard Fergusson said kindly afterwards. "Bad luck you didn't come through". His sentiment not mine.

That autumn when Hitler threatened to take over the Sudetenland, France was bound by treaty to help Czechoslovakia and we France. The British fleet mobilized, war seemed unavoidable. If patriotic belligerence so widespread in 1914 existed anywhere, it should have done so at Sandhurst. In fact I remember the atmosphere among GC's as extremely sombre. One or two spoke in favour of biting the bullet, but most of us must have noticed that the new Boyes anti-tank rifle shown to us on the rifle range (it reputedly had a powerful kick), was only a wooden mock-up. When Chamberlain returned from Munich with peace, at least for a time, the college collectively heaved a sigh of huge relief.

For what everyone now feared must be our last New Year at peace, I joined the family in a small convoy of cars and Military Mission trucks crossing the Suez Canal by pontoon at the Bitter Lake. Turning south into the wastes of Sinai we camped for a night, emerging from the desert some three hundred kilometres later at the tip of the peninsular. Inland a wilderness of massive brown rocks cocked into sizeable hills like a torrent of sugar lumps. Already erected on the sands of a huge bay – a logistical miracle which could have been achieved only by the Camel Corps – stood a large marquee. For a week we all swam, knocked oysters off the rocks and fished for barracuda in the waters of the Red Sea. I told my parents about the boxing debacle, revealing with some pride that I was one of seven or eight juniors in each company to have been selected for promotion. If there was a connection between this and the boxing it did not cross my mind.

The holiday rushed by in a whirl of sport and parties. Characteristically worried that I should know nobody on board the ship home, my mother arranged for a friend returning her fifteen year old daughter to school to invite me to their table. I had met Betty once in Cairo – a quiet girl with shoulder-length dark hair and a pretty face – her father commanded the Irish Guards in the Citadel. We got along well at the table and, thus emboldened, I asked her ashore at Valetta. By Genoa we were slipping out on deck to hold hands by the rail. But my term was about to start and I was booked to travel overland from Marseilles. Suddenly it was our last evening. "Come on with us. Come round through the Bay". But I could not. As the train steamed north towards Lyon I remember staring blindly out of the carriage window, seeing nothing, thinking of her. My first love. And I do not believe we even kissed.

The intermediate term at Sandhurst involved more academic work and military exercises but less drill, preparing us in our senior term for the passing out exam. As a Temporary Corporal I was responsible now not only for myself but for a small section of juniors. Having never been a prefect, or even been at Wellington when my contemporaries were prefects, this was not my métier. On a grey morning in a completely spectator-free stadium in Oxford I did, as a reserve, represent the RMC in an athletics team predictably thrashed by the university. It was the highlight of a rather difficult term. Last but one in the hundred yards.

Every GC possessed a bike and at weekends a fortunate few, like Lord Carrington in the Old Building, could be seen heading in their sports cars for the glamour of 'up to town'. Most weekends I went too, catching a coach from Camberley to Didi's service flat in Kensington. After a weekend spent eating or at the cinema, and a large high tea on the Sunday evening, I would dress again in RMC uniform, take a tube to Piccadilly Circus and catch the 9.00 pm coach back from the Ritz. "You will be all right, dear, won't you?"

Didi usually asked as I reappeared in uniform. I knew exactly what she meant. From corners and doorways all down Piccadilly at least a dozen tarts would come sauntering, hips swinging, towards me. Highly painted, most wore the tart's standard ensemble of a black suit, nipped tightly round a curvaceous bottom, and the inevitable silver fox fur. "Want a good time darling?" Ahead of the alluring smile came an extremely off-putting blast of cheap scent. My resistance was in fact high.

In the spring of 1939 Chamberlain introduced conscription. There was not, for us, to be a senior term, doubts about further promotion or, happily, an exam. We were to be pushed out and commissioned by the summer. "Which did we want?" the staff soon came round asking. "The British Army, Ghurkhas, Indian Army? And which regiment?" Suitors for a regiment's hand had normally to face searching questions from a panel nominated by their prospective 'father-in-law', the Regimental Colonel. A subaltern was paid only £200 a year and on this he could just rub along. Some line regiments, or a corps like the RASC, would accept candidates with nothing more, but the more prestigious infantry regiments and all the cavalry and foot guards required aspirants to have a certain minimum private income. But how much would a man actually *need*? A candidate for the Grenadiers, for example, who had only the regiment's suggested £300 per annum, would have a real struggle when stationed in London. It was a most invidious system.

Happily I knew the regiment I wanted. In Cairo several subalterns from the first battalion of the Royal Northumberland Fusiliers, always known in the army simply as the Fifth, had been Geraldine's regular escorts. Highly regarded by regulars, splendidly manned by Geordies, middle of the road for officers financially, its two battalions had recently been re-equipped and mechanised (as had the Manchester regiment), with the .303 Vickers machine gun, the weapon which had caused such havoc in the last war. The RMC closed in June, 1939. A month later, with two others, I was gazetted into the Fifth.

CHAPTER THREE

AT ELEVEN on a sunny September Sunday morning that every Londoner then alive remembers, all unmarried officers not on duty were clustered around the mess radio at Dover Castle barracks. Six weeks earlier David Brook, Gerry Rickman and I had joined the second battalion of the Fifth. Guests at our first mess night and well wined, we had been initiated into the mess by climbing round the anteroom walls without touching the floor. I had learned to ride a motorbike, been sent away for a week to learn about the army's current bogey, poison gas. Paid eleven shillings a day by the army, with my new £150 allowance I had bought a 1934 Vauxhall family saloon for £37.10.0d, and at every available weekend hurried across Kent to see a girl in Herne Bay on the opposite side of the county. Although very much a new boy, life was good.

Neville Chamberlain had barely stopped speaking when the air raid sirens started. On the dot as usual, these Germans. Actually it was the start of a false alarm that soon sent the whole of London into the shelters. As the wailing stopped a driver arrived from the orderly room. "Colonel's compliments. I am to give you gentlemen a lift to your companies."

We are at war now, I kept thinking to myself as we piled into the fifteen hundredweight, actually at war! The prospect seemed totally unreal. Skirting the castle wall as the driver headed towards the keep, I looked down towards the small town silhouetted far below us against a deep blue swathe of the channel; everything looked so peaceful, the streets entirely deserted. Suddenly a thought came... "colourless, odourless, you probably won't even know it is there...".Whipping out the gas mask everyone carried, I pulled it quickly over my head. Peering around through the goggles I noticed that no one else in the truck was following suit. The mask smelled pretty awful. Hesitating a few moments, acutely embarrassed, I wrenched it off again. Nobody said a word.

At the end of that month the battalion marched out for France. Left behind, we three nineteen-year-old subalterns and whatever stores could not be carried, were to be sent up to the regimental depot in Newcastle. Didi had moved out of London and was renting from my parents' friends, the Rigdens, a house in the village of Stratton Audley, near Bicester, where she would spend the war. Although she never learned to drive, Didi had thereby acquired an asset much coveted at the time. Laden with fifty gallons of petrol bought illicitly from stocks the regiment had left behind, I stopped off for a heartfelt goodbye in north Kent and stored both petrol and the Vauxhall in her garage for the duration. All the family used the car while on leave and, like any other good runner, she sold after the war for four times her purchase price.

The Royal Northumberland Fusiliers had raised a record fifty battalions in 1914-18, and again the red brick barracks at Fenham just north of the Tyne were bursting with trainees. In the mess older officers from the regimental reserve, some of whom had first war medals, cast sceptical eyes over the new influx. As regulars, however, we were rated OK, and more than one Northumbrian landowner would later offer us some shooting.

Ease (crank), Pull (belt), Tap (crank), and resume firing. Under patient sergeant instructors we had virtually to eat and sleep with the Vickers machine gun, not least because of its many potential stoppages. Often illustrated mowing down infantry at close range during the first World War, the Vickers actually performed better at medium ranges of around half a mile, and was reasonably accurate at more than twice that distance. Machine gun companies were allocated to support infantry in much the same way as artillery. The enemy could be engaged indirectly over the heads of our advancing infantry (heaven forefend a loose tripod) or the gun fired 'blind' on fixed lines at night. Gun crews had to know how to use range-finders, and in the expertise it needed the Vickers almost equalled a field gun.

Almost no fighting was going on in France and by November England was under deep snow. The papers began to say that Hitler was comprehensively blockaded: he must be short of raw materials and did not attack simply because he could not. England, we were also told, had no quarrel with the German people, only with Hitler and his Nazis. I could not conjure up much animosity for the German nation as a whole, but the distinction seemed to me even then to be splitting hairs.

As the 'phoney war' continued, recruits began pouring into the depot and surrounding camps. My social life blossomed. For £5 on a sale-and-return basis I bought a comfortable, if unreliable, two-seater Riley off a scrap heap, and at a mess party met Audrey. Her father was Mister Andrews Liver Salts, sales manager for the north of England, who owned a nice terrace house in Newcastle and a small place in Cumberland. After Saturday night dinner and dancing to tunes like 'Run, Rabbit' at the Station Hotel, Newcastle's best, we would push-start the Riley on frozen cobbles in a side street and crawl back to the family sofa on the obligatory side lights.

In April 1940, as Hitler invaded Norway, I was posted to the 9th Battalion, RNF, a newly raised territorial unit with a regular as Commanding Officer. Within days we had crossed to France, ill-equipped and with minimal transport, where we were to continue our training and guard airfields. My company received only four machine guns against its establishment of twelve, eked out by a few Bren guns. Everyone had a .303 rifle, although some of the men had never been on a rifle range. We boasted a single Boyes anti-tank rifle, which no one had actually fired, and one thirty cwt truck for an entire company that was supposed to be motorised. Packed like bullocks into railway wagons (40 hommes, 8 chevaux) the battalion was puffed and shunted from Cherbourg to Le Mans, and from there slowly across northern France to Picardy. Ten days later the Germans entered Belgium. The fog of war descended, circumstances all the more confusing and impenetrable at company level because we had not a single map between us.

It was many years before I discovered from reading what had actually happened. On 17 May, some seventy miles south of the small village of Ferfay, where the 9th Battalion was then guarding a supply dump, the Germans broke through the French 9th Army around St. Quentin. "Ten panzer divisions" Churchill wrote, "aided and supplied by mechanized transport, advanced thirty or forty miles a day.... passed through scores of towns and hundreds of villages without the slightest opposition, their officers looking out of the open cupolas and waving jauntily to the inhabitants". By

May 20th the Germans had reached the sea near Abbeville and turned east up the coast towards Boulogne and Calais. On 19th May my battalion marched a short distance eastwards to guard the airfield at Merville. At dawn on 24th May, somewhat further east in the Belgian border village of Steenbecque, we were attacked *from the west* by German tanks. No wonder we were confused. A final quotation from Churchill – "General Halder, Chief of the German General Staff, has declared that at this moment Hitler made his only effective, direct personal intervention in the battle. At any rate we intercepted a German message sent in clear at 11.42 am on May 24th to the effect that the attack on the line Dunkirk – Hazebrouck – Merville was to be discontinued for the present. Although this order was countermanded next day, Rundstedt would not release the panzers until 26th. Even then he told them not to assault Dunkirk directly".

In Merville we were dive-bombed and for the first time heard the terrifying howl of the Stuka. During a roadside halt soon afterwards an alert sentry grabbed a solitary man in scruffy civilian clothes who came wandering up a gorse-strewn slope from the general direction of Belgium. Overhearing the adjutant ask what incomprehensible language the man was speaking, I suggested Dutch and admitted to knowing some German. (In fact it was probably Walloon). The C.O., a first war veteran, happened to be listening. "He could be a spy," he declared. "Search him for the marks of parachute straps. If he has any – shoot him. If not, let him go". My platoon sergeant led the man away, no doubt feeling almost as sick as I did. Together behind a bush we stripped off the man's shirt. Both of us looked anxiously. No marks. Thank God!

After a long night march, the battalion deployed in the largish village of Steenbecque, shuttered and apparently completely deserted now like everywhere else. Sent forward to look for Germans, my platoon walked warily along the road edges. Nearing a hamlet we deployed prudently into neighbouring fields but came unpleasantly under shellfire from our own twenty-five pounders. Beyond the ridge ahead with its cluster of houses the road fell steeply to a plain. At the bottom of this escarpment, working up the road sides towards us just as we had been doing, we could see several lines of little figures. Shooting started. With our solitary Vickers mounted I had just got off a morale-boosting belt of ammunition when orders came to return to the battalion. That afternoon the Germans attacked Steenbecque with tanks and infantry, continuing until after dark. The battalion withdrew to the next village. All through the following day we waited for the Germans to come again. But for reasons we now know, they did not.

That night the battalion started marching towards the coast, continuing the next, halting in daylight to avoid the Stukas. Aware now that 'Dunkirk' was our destination, we set off on our third consecutive night march with my company at the rear. Sent back to encourage the tail-enders, I joined a small and virtually somnambulist group, which trailed along until we arrived around dawn at a fork. One road went straight ahead. Unaware that the battalion had veered right, we tramped on, exhausted, between ditches now closely packed with abandoned army vehicles. Eventually we found ourselves at the western (Dunkirk) end of the La Panne beach. The battalion, I later learned, had continued to the eastern end, and was embarked from there.

With my group of about ten fusiliers I reported to Corps

headquarters in the end house of a line of respectable beach villas. Officially now 'stragglers', we were told to wait with thousands of others lying up on that much filmed beach. As the sun rose, the noise of an aircraft – they were always German – caused a rather unseemly scramble to the relative safety of the dunes. Returning I saw our corps commander, Sir Alan Brooke, impeccably turned out in service dress with highly polished field boots and glistening spurs, posing nonchalantly on his veranda. Often throughout that day he did this, stiffening many backs, including mine. In the small hours of the following morning my group joined an immense queue which started from the stone Dunkirk mole and stretched far back along the beach. Beyond the mole, as we waited, sometimes shuffling a few yards forward, oil tanks were burning fiercely in Dunkirk's docks. Intermittently there were flashes and explosions of ammunition. Someone up in the queue ahead struck a match and at once there was a bellow "Put out that light!"

By daybreak on 30th May, another sparkling sunny morning, we had progressed to a point on the long mole itself. Men were already starting to peer around, looking anxiously for signs of aircraft which might halt the embarkation. A destroyer came in fast from the sea, manoeuvring quickly against the stone wall perhaps seventy yards ahead of me. The front of the queue began to scramble aboard. With a sudden tremendous clatter, the ship's guns opened up as a bomber flying at little more than mast height missed her with bombs falling close on either side. It flew on with one engine smoking. There was a ripple of cheering.

Helped, and presumably roughly counted by the crew, the line moved slowly forward and I got aboard. No weapons whatever were allowed except revolvers – not even (perhaps mistakenly) the weight of a bren gun. With men packed like penguins on her decks, HMS Vanquisher reversed rapidly, swung around and set off at top speed, jinking most of the way back to avoid torpedoes. I found a place to sit down. The sailors were splendid, stepping endlessly among us with cups of tea.

Grimy, exhausted, some wounded, many who filed ashore at Dover must have been in shock, others as bemused as I was by the sudden transition to quietly ordered normality. After a wash we were given a meal and waiting trains dispersed us slowly across southern England. It was late evening before mine reached Northampton. Officers were allocated to a hotel. I rang Didi at Stratton Audley and after a quickly organised supper went gratefully up to my room. We had marched about two hundred miles; for the last week my boots had scarcely been off my feet. I pulled, the hall porter pulled. Finally he brought a sharp knife. We removed them that way and I slept until the following evening.

The nation hailed the rescue of 338,000 men as a miracle, but the war was now real and on our doorstep. After a week's leave for everyone in the British Expeditionary Force, I rejoined my battalion under canvas in Devon. Within a week or two we had been issued by Ordnance with three times the number of machine guns we had lost in France (hoarded of course when we really needed them), and somewhat more transport. Moved to Norfolk, we set up gun positions along the coast south of Cromer and I was dispatched for further machine gun training to the Small Arms School in Netheravon.

Meanwhile in Kaduna, central Nigeria, Geraldine had married Geoffrey Barton, the Intelligence Officer of my father's brigade and a captain in the Royal Welch Fusiliers. Antony had joined the H.A.C. on the outbreak of war and was now in Aldershot training as an artillery officer. Together we met our burly, fair brother-in-law briefly after the young marrieds arrived back on honeymoon. My father himself, unusual in that he had never served in India, was finally experiencing some of the fruits of empire. From the Commandant's House at Kaduna with its twelve servants, my mother wrote to a friend:."Gerald now has practically a division of troops out here spread over an area as big as Britain. We seem to be always on tour and are off next week thirty-six hours by train to the south, to Lagos where Gerald sits on the Legislative Council, then to the Cameroons. A month in all. We take servants with us and stay at the Governors' or Residents of Provinces' houses. I find it immensely interesting, but very tiring especially in the great heat".

Italy entered the war. I heard at Netheravon that my father's Nigerians, as well as a brigade from the Gold Coast, were to be shipped round Africa to the now strategically important east coast. With well over 300,000 troops in occupied Eritrea, recently conquered Abyssinia and Italian Somaliland, the Italians posed a serious threat, particularly to the Sudan, where they out-numbered our forces by ten to one. An Italian invasion there would threaten General Wavell's vital supply lines to Egypt, both across Africa to Khartoum and up the Red Sea route to Suez. In Kenya too, though protected to some extent by desolate country on her northern frontier, our troops were heavily outnumbered.

Of all this I was, of course, blissfully unaware. Back on the wind-blown beaches at Cromer as the Battle of Britain further south rose to its climax, only monotonous guard duties or more training seemed in prospect. Then I spotted a notice in the company office. Volunteers were again wanted (it was a time of constant re-organisation) this time to officer a machine gun battalion of the King's African Rifles (KAR) in Kenya. I put down my name.

Barely a month later I was on a troopship. Sailing west from Liverpool almost to Newfoundland, we looped unescorted down the American coast, called in at Freetown and took almost a month to round the Cape. Rumours were circulating on board about an armed raider which was loose in the Indian Ocean, but after a week of non-stop hospitality from the ladies of Durban we continued north without incident.

My draft, the first of many, had been narrowly beaten to Kenya by the West Africans. Watching from the rail as our crowded ship finally docked in Mombasa island's beautiful harbour, I heard my name come unexpectedly over the tannoy. Brigadier Smallwood, 'Brig Twig' as he was promptly christened, wanted his son disembarked. Met at the gangplank by a heel-crunching salute from a very black corporal, I was driven off, a pennant flapping importantly on the staff car's bonnet, under the envious eyes of half the troopship. From then until my twenty-first birthday two months later I was to experience in rapid succession all three aspects of Kenya's fascinating geography – its tropical coast, the temperate 'White Highlands' and the bush of the Northern Frontier. Throughout, as is often the case there around Christmas, the weather remained perfect. After England the colony appeared virtually at peace, no food rationing, no bombing and local attempts at a blackout (which disappeared altogether a few months later) were distinctly perfunctory.

My father's Nigerian brigade was under canvas about a hundred miles to the north across the coast road beyond Malindi.

44

Steering clear of local gossip at Lawford's, then Malindi's only hotel, my father himself occupied one of a string of romantic, palm-thatched bungalows whose largish plots, bright with bougainvillea, ran down through a fringe of casuarina trees to the wide sandy foreshore. The best house in picturesque Malindi village belonged to the district officer, the rest to white settlers who used them to escape from the high altitude of their farms. Before and for centuries after 1498, when Vasco da Gama on his way to the Indies 'discovered' the place (and entertained its king with fireworks), Malindi had been a thriving, Arab-influenced port. Now economically a backwater, the local Giriama tribe scratched a subsistence in the tropical scrub of the hinterland. Rated according to one's point of view, bone idle or traditional, their womenfolk added much to the local colour by wearing only beads and a tutu.

After drinks and 'first toasties', as pre-dinner eats were always called, my father brought out his latest hilarious acquisition. Show his pet mongoose a ping-pong ball and he would immediately grab it and shoot it backwards against walls or furniture. The more furiously he kicked the faster this perverse egg bounced back; but he persevered until we ourselves grew tired of the racket. The staff brought us supper and we went early to bed with our Dietz lamps.

To rejoin my draft at the Nairobi transit camp, I booked a few days later on the night sleeper from Mombasa. A single line ran 500 miles through the highlands to Kisumu on Lake Victoria, and the train took ten hours to Nairobi. Showering wood sparks, we puffed ponderously up the wooded coastal hills so slowly that, missing the train in Mombasa on a later occasion, we overhauled it two stops up the line in a taxi. I woke next morning in the total blackness of a little wooden sleeping compartment feeling (as

45

always) claustrophobic, and let up the blind. Goodness knows what I expected. Wild life photography and television had not then preset one's expectations. Outside was bright, sparkling morning. Across a huge expanse of fawn-coloured grassland, broken here and there by deep dongas lined with flat-topped thorn trees, herds of many different animals were grazing. Antelope, zebra, giraffe, all in such prodigious numbers it seemed like a conjuring trick. I just sat and gaped.

My mother, who had recently arrived in Kenya, was living that December of 1940 in the white residential suburb of Muthaiga. Geraldine had just produced her first born, Tim, in a Nairobi hospital. Having local connections I was quickly released from the drab surroundings of Nairobi transit camp and moved in the usual colonial style into a club. Nairobi Club on what settlers then called 'The Hill', the Government quarter, drew its membership mainly from Government employees and business. I joined the Muthaiga Country Club, home-from-home for the better-off white settlers, which had always offered military membership to officers seconded to the K.A.R. In the men's bar a burly, fair-haired man seemed to attract much attention. Lord Erroll would be murdered the following month and the reputation of his decadent, self-centred, moneyed clique, tipped publicly on to the dunghill.

Soon posted to the 1/3 (pronounced First/Third) K.A.R., a regular unit that always recruited in the colony, I found my battalion camped under the shadow of Mt Kenya beside a dusty murram road running north from Nanyuki. Days later an hospitable local settler offered to mount a few officers for a morning's hunting. Four or five of us assembled soon after dawn at a rocky outcrop on his large ranch. Some locals had turned out too, the farmer himself wearing a proper hunting jacket, green I think, and looking business-like. We cantered off through sparse leleshwa scrub across a seemingly boundless plain of short grass. To our east the sun rose abruptly above the snow peaks of the great mountain. A few of the foxhounds chased something – a duiker probably – then lost it. We sat around on our ponies, waiting. I talked to another officer, also pink and white from England, about 'after the war'. He said he planned to expand his father's laundry business, in which he had already worked for a while, and make lots of money. (I thought this exotic but secretly, not quite the thing.) Nothing really happened. Above us the twin peaks of the mountain glistened through a circlet of white cloud. There was game everywhere – herds of wildebeest and the black striped Thomson's gazelle. Now and then a hare or a dik-dik would bolt away through the short scrub. It grew quite hot. As the scent faded a hound would collapse, tongue lolling in the shade of a bush, until the African hunt whip cracked him out again.

Gradually I took in this scene. The beauty and wonder of it began to mount in me. So much space, the brilliant light, banks of cumulus cloud now gathering on a huge sweep of the horizon. Here was untrammelled nature, immemorial, everlasting. This was the world, I thought, as it should be. Forget the war, to hell with civilisation! Kenya was the place. It was a feeling that, all these years later, I can still recapture

Back in the real world the war soon swept us up. In January 1941 two divisions of Indian troops under General Platt in the Sudan invaded Eritrea. After heavy fighting in hugely mountainous country they reached Asmara, the capital, then the Red Sea at Masawa, on 8 April. Simultaneously, but over twelve hundred miles away to the southeast, two African divisions under General Cunningham entered Italian Somaliland. One advanced up the coast to take Mogadishu. With my father's Nigerian brigade in the lead it swept at record speed across the barren Somaliland lowlands, 744 miles in seventeen days, to reach the Abyssinian highlands at Jijiga. There the Italians briefly attempted a stand. Captured British Somaliland was rapidly retaken, and on 6th April this same division entered Addis Ababa.

Further to the west near Lake Rudolf in Kenya, the second African division, and a division of white South African troops, to which my machine gun battalion was initially attached, advanced into the remote, mountainous south of Abyssinia. Although their progress was slower, by mid-May the two parts of General Cunningham's force had joined hands near the central Abyssinian lakes. Haile Selassie, who since 1936 had been in exile in England, re-entered his capital in triumph. Stiffened by German successes in Libya, it took a further six months to overcome Italian resistance in the rugged country around the source of the Blue Nile at Lake Tana. But the triumphant campaign which had been planned by General Wavell from Cairo was effectively over. The Duke of Aosta finally surrendered in November and died later in captivity.

In the middle of January, with each truck keeping dust distance from the one in front, our battalion convoy wound slowly down the escarpment north of Nanyuki. As we descended below four thousand feet, thin grass shrivelled into brown wisps in the sandy soil and occasional stunted trees were replaced by almost continuous thorn scrub. Warm became hot. Camping that night on the banks of the Uaso Nyero, where elephant came down to water in what is now a game park, we set off next morning into the rocky bush country of the Northern Frontier District.

Like all more senior officers at that stage of the war, our C.O. and my company commander, Mrefu ('the tall one') Kelly, son of a very distinguished admiral, were regulars who had served for some years with the K.A.R. All the remaining officers in my company were ex-farmer settlers who had trained in the local white territorial unit, the Kenya Regiment. Mute despite working at my Swahili each afternoon, I found everyone helpful over the language. Most of the askaris who paraded barefoot in their well-pressed khaki tunics and shorts could not communicate with one another either, except in this lingua franca. Recognising members of my platoon off parade was another problem. By the time we left camp I had begun to associate a few of the faces that grinned at me during the day with tribes. Teeth sharpened to points meant a Mkamba. Mulwa, my orderly, was one, as were nearly all the drivers. Inexplicably they arrived from the dry plains east of Nairobi with an intuitive grasp of things mechanical. Finer features and facial scar marks could be a Nandi, probably with a name beginning 'Kip', from the mountainous western highlands; they made excellent soldiers and now, to the world's admiration, make superb athletes. Blacker skinned with more negroid features – and I was assured, spectacular penises – had to be a Luo from around Lake Victoria. Fighting qualities apparently somewhat suspect....

Fully motorised, the battalion headed up the east of Lake Rudolf, emerging from bush country on to a coruscating dead-flat, treeless salt pan which shimmered with mirage as far ahead as one could see. The Chalbi desert was passable only in dry weather. Anxious not to get stuck we raced each other across its fragile crust, sometimes five abreast, halting on the other side in the cool oasis of North Horr. Word came that the South Africans fighting up ahead were sending back some prisoners, who included the Italian district commissioner at Mega, an important regional capital just across the border. In a colonial gesture that seemed even then bizarre, our C.O. decided his officers must entertain this official to dinner.

Every morning, at 7.50 am precisely, tens of thousands of chirping sand grouse would sweep in from the desert, settle like a brown skirt across the waterholes to drink, and after a few minutes swirl into the air and disappear. Disgracefully I 'browned' a flock of them on the water. Fourteen little birds from one cartridge of my new shotgun fed the mess at dinner. Next day our guest contrived an even more futile gesture by escaping (temporarily) on the way south.

As the days passed I found the soles of my feet becoming increasingly sore. Finally it became painful even to pull on boots and I reported sick. The M.O. took an amused look, then sent me off to sit under a tree. Digging expertly with a needle, an African orderly unearthed no fewer than nineteen jiggers, an insanitary little insect of dry areas which likes to burrow to lay its eggs. A little lamp paraffin dropped into each nest hole killed off the eggs. I had to slop around in slippers for a few days, but learned never again to put foot to the tent floor without a sandal.

CHAPTER FOUR

THE SOUTH Africans alone captured Mega, the key hilltop town that blocked our only road into the interior. As we mounted our guns against counter-attack 3,000 feet up on the sparse grass of the mountain top, several hundred Italian prisoners squatted resignedly outside the great wooden doors of a crenelated stone fort – by far the largest building we had seen since leaving Nairobi. Beyond, in the alleys of a sizeable native township, all the dwellings looked mean, square and squat, crudely constructed of uneven boulders and draped with dishevelled thatch; not a patch, we thought, on Kenya's native rondavels. Their hirsute inhabitants appeared ragged and unkempt too, but with no language in common, our askaris could not communicate. It was raining steadily, the fort half hidden in cloud and the temperature at least thirty degrees below that of the plain. We did not think much of Ethiopia.

At this juncture the South African division was withdrawn to be sent to Egypt and my company attached to a brigade of East African troops that took up what soon became a pursuit. After invading Abyssinia five years earlier the Italians had built some good roads and established garrisons at strategic points. Thereafter, to judge by the photographs we found, their troops had settled down comfortably to co-habit with the local women. Rapid British advances up Italian Somaliland, the first in the war, were making news headlines in Britain, but it was soon obvious that our own brigade's movement northwards was too slow to be interesting. This was not because of the Italians, who were usually obliging enough to withdraw as soon as fired upon, or sooner. The mountainous country through which we were moving was totally undeveloped. A single-track earth road wound through scrub-filled valleys, unmetalled and, when it rained, virtually impassable. While we heard nothing about ourselves, or our own sector of operations, there were constant references on the BBC World Service to the returning Emperor, Haile Selassie, and the exploits of his, to us mythical, 'revolting Abyssinians'. No doubt we were jealous, but the description seemed peculiarly apt.

When finally the Italians made a stand it was on a large hill overlooking the road, which was loosely covered with small trees and bush and marked on the map as 'Soroppa'. With impressive bang-bangs ('a brilliant little action' the official account later called it) the brigade attacked from three sides. It was not machine gun country. With no target visible my platoon and its guns were sent to struggle on foot up a long slope with the infantry. Lacking the first courage of inexperience I found it scary after France. Visibility was only yards; if anyone were waiting on the summit … Fortunately the Italians could be relied upon. We had just re-mounted our guns on the now deserted hilltop when an observant askari spotted movement in a clearing well ahead. He opened fire. As we later discovered, he achieved our only confirmed hit of the campaign. One dead donkey.

Playing grandmother's footsteps with the weather, the brigade inched northwards. Often, as the fragile road surface steamed after a sudden shower, everything must halt for the rest of the day. Addis was taken, the front moved on. Late in May we finally struggled onto a wide, metalled road beside the Djibouti-Addis railway, and moved into former Italian barracks at Diredawa.

Our 'boys', or personal servants, were Kenyan civilians fed by the army but employed and paid privately by British officers or the handful of British non-commissioned officers in a K.A.R. company. Mine was on loan from a settler captain, who now returned from leave bringing a handsome, but inexperienced Somali youth who wanted to go back home. I was myself due some leave. The quickest way back to Kenya was now the long way around. So Omar Botan and I caught a convoy going north-eastwards to Berbera on the coast of recently recaptured British Somaliland. There we found a boat across to Aden, then another round the Horn of Africa to Mombasa, and finally travelled by train up to Nairobi. In all, a journey of some two thousand miles.

In 1941 only generals travelled by air. After three weeks with my mother and Geraldine in their rented house at Muthaiga I reported once more to Nairobi transit camp. Convoys of South African Chev 3-tonners left for Abyssinia twice a week carrying stores and personnel. Like the friend who amazed Churchill by leaving for the front in 1914 without a valet, I lacked an indispensable item. Our excellent Cape-coloured driver obligingly stopped a moment in dusty Isiolo; Omari bundled up all his worldy possessions in thirty seconds and scrambled over the tailgate. Long safaris in convoy were à la mode that year. Officers fortunately sat in front, but I remember my damp rumpled shorts sticking to the shiny brown Rexine of over-firm bench seats, the endless juddering of corrugations. Sometimes a truck crawled so slowly through deep potholes that the bucketing vehicle would be overtaken by its own dustcloud. The passengers behind, enveloped and choking with dust, would bang on the cab roof and yell for respite. Mostly convoys kept up a steady pace around twenty m.p.h., stopping briefly on the hour and for longer at midday. The greater the heat the colder became the water in our dripping canvas chargals. They hung from an outside mirror strut and were cooled by evaporation.

Between four and five o'clock the convoy leader would pull off the track near a source of water. Personal boys brought washing water, made an instant fire and a mug of tea. Camp beds and mosquito nets were erected, tents rarely needed. Rations were usually either Fray Bentos' agreeable corned beef or mushy, tin-tasting M and V, a meat and veg stew as unimaginative as its name. On safari officers and any British NCO messed together. Guinea fowl, the yellow-necked francolin or a dik-dik being usually around, we were rarely without one or the other.

Back at Diredawa in September I found my company packing up to move. We were not, as we had expected, to join the final assault on Gondar, which would end the campaign. In French Somaliland the authorities had a sizeable army and supported the government in Vichy. We badly needed the port at Djibouti to relieve intense pressure on Aden, but the French threatened to blow it up if attacked. Our only option to enforce compliance was to blockade. British Somaliland lay along one border and the recently captured Italian colony of Eritrea along the other. My company was to be based at Assab on Eritrea's Red Sea coast.

Skirting drab and treeless Addis Ababa, where swarms of Habash tarts regularly overwhelmed the defences of the transit camp, we camped ten miles further on and received our final orders. Northwards, a magnificent new Italian-built flint road climbed spectacularly into the mountains. Fascist insignia were carved every few miles into the rock face, and at the top of the 8,000 ft pass a tablet announced once again that Mussolini had *'per la strada una passione romana'*. Mussolini Pass divided the bleak upland plateau on which Addis is built from the mountainous district of Dessie. Descending 5,000 feet in under twenty miles, we wound through fertile valleys dotted with maize plantations and flanked by green hills rising almost sheer on either side. At 8.00 am one morning outside a place called Batie, the askaris huddled in their greatcoats at the top of an immense escarpment separating mountainous Ethiopia from the Eritrean plain. Coiled below us, ten miles of continuously snaking 'S' bends plunged from a chilly 5,000 feet to the desert floor at sea level.

Our second task smacked of pre-war soldiering in Palestine. As well as contributing to the blockade of French Somaliland, we were to secure communications between Batie and the port of Assab, which lay three hundred miles to the north-east beyond the dead flat, barren Danakil desert. For many years Wajerati (bandits) operating in country to the west had raided regularly across the Assab-Batie road to take arms and cattle from the equally ferocious Danakil tribes on the French Somaliland border. The Italian authorities had usually sided with the settled Danakil, who were now actively helping us with our blockade. We too had to protect them against intrusion by their old enemy, and at the same time guard the road.

As we descended the escarpment the temperature rose perceptibly with every mile. Mounting some of our twelve machine guns on their special truck fittings, we set off from the bottom along a blistering, ruler-straight, dead flat macadam road towards the solitary oasis at Sardo, a hundred and fifty miles away. Twenty minutes later a truck tyre exploded like a gunshot. Soon afterwards three others did the same and we learned to inflate them when cold only to five pounds pressure. Approaching Assab the road was still littered with burnt-out Italian lorries, the victims of trainee bomber pilots from Aden. Assab itself was undamaged, its whitewashed colonial-style bungalows well equipped with fans and comfortable to live in. Some Italian colonists were still at work under British supervision. Here, as in Abyssinia, we felt they diminished themselves and our superior European culture by co-habiting so openly with the primitive locals.

At Assab a squadron of the East African Armoured Car Regiment was available to help us with the blockade. Neither armoured cars nor we could function properly off the road, nor was wireless equipment available that would operate over the three hundred miles involved. It was therefore decided to put a machine gun platoon and some armoured cars up at Batie and the same at Sardo, where there was water, operating road patrols between them. The rest of us would stay on in popular Assab. There the askaris were enjoying exciting new experiences, first in seeing, and then tentatively bathing in the sea, and a familiar one in making full use of the local talent. All of them except Omari who (aged about seventeen) had already contrived to catch VD in Addis.

A fortnight later a frightened supply lorry driver reported at Sardo that a large body of Wajerati was approaching the oasis. Our platoon commander there was unfortunately away on patrol. The armoured car officer left in command knew he must act quickly: in an hour the Wajerati would have watered and been away across the road. Taking a detachment of our riflemen and two Vickers guns mounted on open trucks under command of a British NCO, the officer drove up the raised tarmac road into the middle of the large oasis, which covered at least fifty acres. Someone, whether he or the British NCO, then foolishly fired a warning burst over the heads of several hundred Wajerati scattered among the palm trees. In the ensuing gun battle our machine gunners found themselves perched like ducks in a shooting gallery. One truck managed to dismount its gun but the crew were soon disabled. In the end only five men, a third of the detachment, got away. A machine gun, subsequently recovered, and rifles were taken. Hours later reinforcements sent from Assab found the Wajerati long gone. Strewn around, some clearly having struggled vainly to crawl away, were the bodies of ten askaris. All of them, including the wounded, had been castrated.

By chance I met the vehicle bringing in these unfortunates. Two of the askaris were still alive. I saw a man lean over to commiserate with one of them, a fellow Mkamba. The young man lifted a corner of the blanket covering him to show his friend what had been done and shook his head. Life must have seemed totally unbearable; he wanted to die. Both the injured did so that night in hospital.

Bombers were summoned from Aden but to no avail. The Wajerati had vanished. Our new company commander, a settler named Johnnie Nimmo, was told to move the whole company except a platoon at Batie into the former Italian hospital at Sardo. This was a substantial whitewashed stone building around a central courtyard; the Italians having as usual built with an eye to defence, the courtyard was protected by a thick wall with rifle embrasures.

A British political officer was based with the Sultan of the Danakil near the frontier at Abroborofaghi. It was only forty miles away so we could keep in constant touch by wireless.

Isolated in desert temperatures that regularly exceeded 40 degrees C we welcomed the hospital's high ceilings. My three brother officers were now all ex-settlers and Johnnie spoke Kikuyu as well as Swahili. In siesta time I worked for, and eventually passed, the government's lower standard Swahili exam, for which the army paid a modest £10. The much more difficult Higher warranted £50, but as ours was not a Tanganyika-raised battalion (where they spoke the language properly) everyone in 1/3 KAR spoke only superior 'kitchen'. Sadly the denser thickets of Swahili prefixes would remain permanently beyond me.

On large shallow marshes near Abroborofaghi thousands of duck and Egyptian geese cannot previously have been shot at. Once or twice a week around dawn the Political Officer and I would wade thigh-deep into the warm water with two askaris apiece, leaving a line of men on each bank to act as beaters. As one line advanced, the birds would circle quite low above us, then settle again behind ... and obligingly vice-versa. The Africans loved it – lumps of good meat coming splosh into the water every few minutes. Our retrievers waded around excitedly until we had gathered about sixty. With these and an occasional buck from the nearby plains, we kept the troops reasonably well supplied with meat. Lack of green vegetables was partly offset by scurvy tablets, but several of us developed quite nasty veldt sores.

It was the more avoidable sores of gonorrhoea that came nearest to crippling the company. From day one the native village below the hospital walls began to mushroom. The MO soon reported a sharp increase in VD, Johnnie put the village out of bounds and bussed out any obviously unattached females to Assab. A fortnight later two women were caught scaling the hospital walls. By now we knew that, one way or another, virtually all of the askaris were involved from the sergeant-major downward. By the mores of the time an officer could not be seen to search a native hut. Threatening draconian punishment for more unreported VD, we held what must have been a highly unusual 'private parts' inspection for the entire company. Almost half of the men were infected. Things improved after this, but it was just as well we were not required for active service.

After two months with no sign of Wajerati an armoured car reconnaissance patrol came unexpectedly on a large band of them at a waterhole. Following orders to take revenge, they attacked at once and killed sixty. On their way out the last of the three South African-made vehicles stuck in a hole. The other two cars were out of ammunition and could only rush back to base for reinforcements. For a desperate half hour, so the crew commander told me, Wajeratis were climbing and banging on their turret, trying to poke rifle muzzles through the slits. The crew knew what had happened to our askaris. They also knew, which the Wajerati did not, that rifle fire concentrated on one spot would penetrate the armoured car's makeshift armour. The European driver became hysterical and had forcibly to be prevented from shooting himself. But all fortunately survived.

In January 1942, with the Japs now in the war and the navy at Aden much too busy to continue a blockade, we were ordered back to Kenya. French Somaliland came over to the allies at the end of that year when Madagascar surrendered. Our scattered battalion was to reassemble as a unit at Gilgil, west of Nairobi in the Rift Valley, and it was rumoured we were to be converted into an armoured car regiment.

During a farewell visit to Assab there was a rare downpour of rain. Mulwa, my orderly, womanising in the native township, told me that the hut he was in, and most of the others around, had liquefied slowly into a circle of bare bamboos. One episode from our month-long safari southwards still sticks in my mind. During a rest day in southern Abyssinia, bored and no doubt looking for plaudits for topping up the pot, I set off with Omari, Mulwa and my recently acquired 8mm Mannlicher rifle to look for a buck. I was no sort of marksman, but after a longish trek across stony bush country we finally spotted, standing on the next ridge, the tall straight horns of a pair of oryx. These were much bigger animals than any I had shot before, the size of a horse, dark grey and within easy range. As one of them fell, Omari, who never seemed to pray to Mecca but was a stickler for this particular ritual, dashed forward, whooping, and quickly cut its throat. Both the Africans were cock-a-hoop. They skinned the large, well-fed carcase and cut off one massive hind haunch. It was all they could carry. Omari asked if I wanted the horns, which were at least three feet long, ringed – annulated I believe is the correct term – and highly elegant. But what on earth could I do with them? Keep them in my tent? Vultures were already circling over great heaps of wasted flesh. "No, let's go" I said. Increasingly uncomfortable about this self-indulgent incident, I went permanently off buck shooting and the following year sold my rifle.

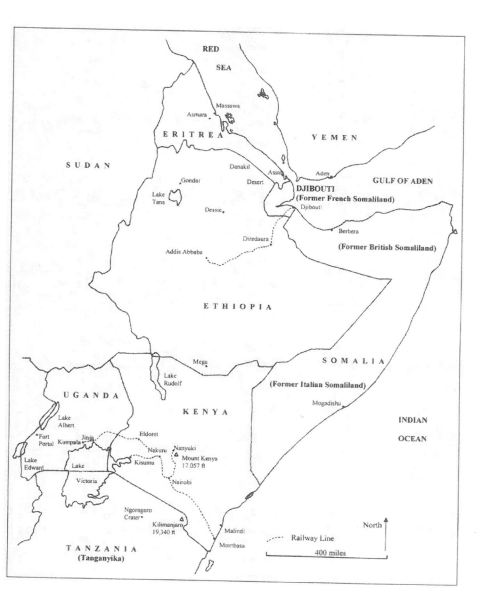

RED
SEA

Massawa

Asmara

ERITREA

YEMEN

SUDAN

Danakil
Desert

Aden

GULF OF ADEN

Gondar

Assab

Lake
Tana

DJIBOUTI
(Former French Somaliland)

Djibouti

Dessie

Berbera

Diredaura

(Former British Somaliland)

Addis Abbaba

ETHIOPIA

Mega

SOMALIA

Lake
Rudolf

(Former Italian Somaliland)

UGANDA

KENYA

Lake
Albert

Mogadishu

INDIAN

Fort
Portal

Jinja

Eldoret

OCEAN

Kampala

Nakuru

Nanyuki

Lake
Edward

Kisumu

Mount Kenya
17,057 ft

Lake

Victoria

Nairobi

Ngorogoro
Crater

North

Kilimanjaro
19,340 ft

Malindi

Railway Line

TANZANIA
(Tanganyika)

Mombasa

400 miles

Eastern Africa

61

At Gilgil we found the battalion camped in a big grass clearing amongst the leleshwa a mile from the town. In the township itself a straggling row of Indian-run dukas lined one side of the earth road, which was then Kenya's principal east-west highway. With so many troops and service vehicles now in the neighbourhood, clouds of red murram dust swept repeatedly into the open shop fronts, settling in layers on the rows of tins that lined the shelves and filming the glass tops of the display counters. Behind the shops' corrugated iron roofs were small plots carefully screened for use of the Indian shop owners' wives and families. Behind these the single-track railway ran westwards to Lake Victoria. From Gilgil a thirty-mile rail spur branched north, climbed the escarpment out of the Rift Valley at the township boundary and ended just beyond the equator at Thomson's Falls. Along the road to the escarpment were dozens of military notices and clusters of wooden huts. This small, dusty junction had become a sizeable wartime cantonment.

Living conditions in Kenya at the beginning of 1942 were much as they must have been pre-war. The eighty-mile journey from Gilgil to Nairobi on a pot-holed main road could take anything from five hours to two days depending on whether it was raining on the Kijabe escarpment. Gangs of Italian POW had already begun blasting there for a better alignment, and the Nairobi-Nakuru road would soon be tarmac. This of course changed everything.

Settlers still on their farms maintained a local tradition of generous hospitality. About thirty miles north of our campsite a small spur projected from the 15,000 foot Aberdare mountain range into the grass plain below. The triangle of green, well-wooded and watered farmland thus enclosed was already becoming notorious as the Happy Valley. With one or two favoured older officers I found myself invited to Kipipiri at weekends. Somewhere in her late thirties, Mary Miller had two children, now approaching teenage, by her first husband, Jock Leslie-Melville, who had been killed before the war in a riding accident. Her second husband had been the first officer casualty in Abyssinia and she was doubtless lonely. Arriving at Mary's whitewashed farmhouse on a Friday evening, a hipbath would be filled in front of a blazing cedar wood fire in one's bedroom and everybody changed into a dressing gown for a candlelit dinner. (This agreeable Kenya practice had already caught out my parents: of course 'changing' in the thirties normally meant a dinner jacket). Mary had a dairy herd, but any farming she did seemed remarkably relaxed. She had no telephone and to get mail from the PO box in Gilgil, or deliver a message, she would send a uniformed sais twenty miles on a pony. If one of our party was not alone between the linen sheets of Mary's comfortable beds, any co-habiting was so discreet (or I was so naive) I never noticed it.

Leslie-Melville had been the colony's highest handicapped polo player, and Mary still kept his private pack of foxhounds. Before breakfast on a brilliant Saturday morning I would ride out behind them on to the great, dun plain. With Mary's black huntsman in charge the pack was supposed to hunt only jackal, and generally did so. If remotely hard-pressed their quarry always dived down a convenient antbear hole. Hounds then became distracted by the innumerable buck running across their scent and ended up catching nothing at all. But what fun it was!

After a fortnight I received a deeply worried letter from my mother and went down to Nairobi. Antony's field regiment of gunners had been part of the ill-fated 18th Division which reached

Singapore only after the Japanese had invaded. Pushed straight up into Malaya they had been outflanked and overwhelmed by the bicycle-riding Japs, just as we had been by the Germans. Passionate about her family and perhaps especially about Antony (who was so like her own father), my mother knew he had got back to Singapore, was in hospital with malaria when the Japs entered. After that, not a word. Geraldine was living with her at the time and my father, now a major-general and G.O.C. in Southern Rhodesia, came up when he could, but there was nothing anyone could say to lift the black cloud of anxiety she very rarely mentioned.

While the battalion awaited delivery of our new armoured cars from South Africa, Johnnie Nimmo, himself a useful polo player, introduced me to David Begg. A friendly, middle-aged Scot and kingpin of local polo, he managed the large sheep station surrounding Gilgil township, then owned by Sir John Ramsden. Near his unpretentious wooden bungalow David had put up a *makuti* (palm) roofed shack, a few benches and some goal posts to make an extremely dusty, but well patronised, private polo ground. I bought an experienced pony from him for £20, and graduating a great deal too rapidly from knocking a ball around the camp, joined local farmers for practice chukkas.

I had yet to fly when my father, who sometimes stood in for Sir William Platt as C-in-C in East Africa, suggested I join him on an inspection visit to Mombasa. Five of us filled a small two-engined Rapide. On the way back one of its engines began to cough, then briefly failed. The pilot said he must put down at the only refuelling point in three hundred miles of rocky bush country between the coast and Nairobi. Taking off again from a runway designed at best for very small private planes, he backed the tail as far as possible

64

into the bush. We shot violently forward. Ahead I could see necks tauten and hands clamp, as mine had, on our seat arms. At the last second the pilot jerked back the stick. We cleared the line of trees ahead by inches. Not a word was said afterwards.

Our hot, cumbersome armoured cars arrived and askaris were trained to drive them. Our first field exercise unfortunately coincided with the onset of the rains; like most of the squadron, mine spent the night in a ditch. Sent soon afterwards for a course at the East African Command Tactical School based in a hutted camp a mile from the local polo ground, I found the emphasis was now all on the Japanese and jungle warfare. None of the lecturers had direct experience of jungle and no films were available. The most striking exhibit on the course was, in fact, the school's new commandant, a Colonel Catt. A regular officer in the Scots Guards, said to be resting from arduous service in Cyrenaica, and an expert (we noted) in desert navigation, the colonel electrified a predominantly war service audience by his staccato mode of speech and highly polished parade ground appearance. Large moustaches sprouted like spring rhubarb from the sides of a steeply tilted guardee cap and he was said to be a notable martinet. Back in camp I was surprised to be told by my C.O. that the commandant would like me back at the Tactical School as his adjutant. Knowing this made me a captain, I gladly accepted.

In the event Philip Catt proved both kindly and undemanding. Probably he was a deeply disappointed man, but I was much too young, self-centred and bewitched by the local life to get to know him. The African population locally had yet to be 'enlightened' by what the askari would see overseas. Settlers up country could still go away for days at a time while leaving all their doors unlocked.

Theft was very rare and nothing, not even petrol, was rationed. Most Friday afternoons I would take my elderly Chev panel van fifty miles through Nakuru up to Spencer and Lilian Tryon's long, rambling bungalow above Molo station. Spencer, lean and wiry in his seventies, was the colony's best-known horse coper; Lilian, rather younger, hailed originally from the Bicester country. There was a long drop loo in the garden and usually a saddle or two dumped in the drawing room chairs. Out at daybreak on their grass downs I could watch a string of racehorses on the gallops, or the African head groom, almost as skilful a horseman as Spencer himself, bring along one pony after another as he schooled a bunch for polo. Next day they would mount me for Sunday polo at the Molo club.

That Christmas I joined a three-car family party for the long trip to Fort Portal and the Mountains of the Moon in Western Uganda. Heading south round Lake Edward where we saw large herds of elephant, we put the cars on a steamer plying down Lake Kivu to Costermansville (now Bukavu) capital of the Belgian Congo province of Ruanda-Urundi. Swahili was spoken and I asked the African steering our sizeable ship how much the company paid him. "The equivalent of fifteen shillings", he replied, "per month." The Belgian authorities were strongly pro-Vichy. When, stupidly, I asked for *'Petrole, s'il-vous-plait'* at a garage instead of *'essence'* the *sal Belge* promptly put in kerosene. The car had to be towed back.

Early in 1943 I was an umpire for a Command exercise to simulate the jungle warfare for which we were preparing. Deep in native plots high with maize and plantains in a remote native reserve to the east of Mount Kenya, my bowels began, as I thought, to tell me I had pinched too many bananas. However Nairobi General, the military hospital to which I was eventually admitted, diagnosed amoebic dysentery, probably contracted in Abyssinia. Soon the undignified treatment became all too familiar: Emetine (or was it Yateren?) by mouth in the morning, Yateren (or maybe Emetine) by the back passage at 5.00 pm. The latter must be held ("as long as you can now"), and when discharged with an uncomfortable burning sensation would, hopefully, be full of little amoebae. Everyone from the ward sister downwards seemed intensely interested in my stools.

Staying afterwards on sick leave with my mother and Geraldine I collected her mail one morning at the Muthaiga Club. Stuck to the noticeboard was a yellow telegram: Antony had been listed a POW. Much excited I rushed back to the house. "*Marvellous news –* Antony is safe – he is a prisoner!" My mother took one wide-eyed look at the telegram and passed out cold on the parquet floor. "Idiot", Geraldine muttered as my mother gradually came to on the sofa. "How could you?" In fairness I had not fully realised what a whole year of writing twice weekly and consigning letters and parcels into the void must have meant to her. Rumours had already begun to circulate about the Japs' brutal treatment of their prisoners, but I suspect nothing after this was quite as bad as the corroding uncertainty of that first year.

Unfortunately my amoebae proved rather deeply attached. Optimistically posted back to regimental duty, I spent six weeks with 2/3 KAR training for Burma on the Athi plains south-east of Nairobi, and thereafter succumbed again to dysentery. Omari too went into the native hospital where sadly he died from tuberculosis the following year. Successive desk jobs as a staff captain ended even more quickly and eventually I found myself on a hospital ship bound for the recuperative cold of an English winter.

It was late in 1943, the battle for Italy just beginning. Passing through the Suez canal our converted cruise liner steamed along a silent, blacked-out Mediterranean with the large red crosses on her sides floodlit and every porthole ablaze. Strolling on deck with the nurses after a dinner dance we were positively encouraged to talk loudly. Of course I wasn't ill – it seemed surreal. At Malta the ship took on casualties – some had been wounded, more were suffering from poliomyelitis then raging, or diseases like Malta fever – and sailed placidly home to Southampton.

After some weeks in a Dorset hospital I was posted, still in a low medical category, to the Fusiliers' wartime depot at Chester. Sick leave and a three hundred mile petrol allowance provided the chance to travel around. It was now the spring of 1944. With the end of the blitz I found bomb damage in central London much less noticeable than it had been in 1940. The stock in the shops surprised me. Of course there were shortages of matches, watches, some torch batteries, razor blades (dull blades we renovated in a glass of water) but there was a much greater range of clothing and shoes, both of course rationed, more books and non-luxury items than I had expected. Most London restaurants could provide a better three-course meal than in Nairobi for the authorised maximum charge of 5 shillings, to which upmarket places added a house charge. Rail goods traffic had greatly increased, passenger trains and buses were consistently overcrowded. People complained of trains being unpunctual, but during a dozen journeys none of mine was more than fifteen minutes late. In Oxfordshire, where I stayed with Didi, pony traps were common, yet friends living barely ten miles apart had often not met for months. What impressed me most however, coming home from a military backwater, was the sheer scale of things – streets thronged with allied troops, the roar of big aircraft, talk of corps where we had thought in battalions.

Peter, son of my wine-merchant great-uncle John Russell, had qualified as a chartered accountant, become a bomber pilot and sadly been shot down into the North Sea the previous year. Often needing a bed in London, I would stay with his widow Norah – now a director, and later the eminent chairman of Chatto and Windus – in her book-crammed flat in Vincent Square. One Sunday morning I woke there to the unusual noise of anti-aircraft fire. A front page article in the Evening Standard just the previous evening had described the first of Hitler's pilotless V1 bombers to reach London. When the steady drone of an approaching engine suddenly cut out I knew to dive under the blankets and pull a pillow over my head. There was a splintering crash, the room was showered with broken glass. Norah was all right, but all the windows at the back had gone – clearly she could do without a visitor. In uniform at the Park Lane Hotel, then much frequented by the army as a transit hotel, they said a room was available on the ninth floor. Somewhat flustered, I was dismayed to hear myself blurt "You don't have one a bit lower down, do you?" They did not. For most people the approaching drone of a doodle-bug and awaiting its cut out were much more nerve-racking than the silent potential of a V2, which followed later. As the V2 campaign progressed one came to accept an occasional bang as a fact of life.

After a certain period of time an unfit officer would lose his acting rank. It was thus as a measly lieutenant that I went on a six-week staff course at the former RMC, Sandhurst. With about a hundred others I was given a room only a few paces from mine of five years earlier. We learned the roles of different military formations in the Order of Battle, and in late hours of homework prepared plans to shift brigades and divisions to fight paper battles devised by the staff. I found this very stimulating and soon afterwards was ordered to report for interview to the Operations Department of the War Office.

My father happened at this time to be briefly in London from Madagascar, where he was G.O.C. After telling him over lunch about this potential new job at the War Office – and characteristically receiving his good wishes but absolutely no advice – I walked round to Whitehall. It was a key moment. My interviewer, a surprisingly young major-general, explained that the vacancy was for a staff captain in his department. His department was responsible for planning military operations in North-West Europe, where our forces were currently held up in the bocage countryside of Normandy following the landings. Did I want the job?

Often over the years I have wondered how life would have changed had I simply replied what, in retrospect, duty and even commonsense so obviously required: "Thank you, Sir". Instead the twenty-four year old babbled on about promotion prospects, wanting to go abroad again and make use of his (unremarkable) German. The general gave me one sharp look and said that something could no doubt be arranged.

CHAPTER FIVE

MY POSTING when it came seemed quite exciting: a captain on the planning staff for the newly formed Control Commission to rule Germany after her surrender. The Commission's offices in West London were accessible by tube from Marble Arch. Granny Gertrude's Park West flat was conveniently on the Edgware Road and I found myself a bed-sit nearby. On a course in Brighton to learn about Nazi organisations I got to know a large, fair captain slightly younger than myself just down from Oxford; at work in London he always appeared highly organised. Michael Pocock and his wife, Nina, living in her parents' Wimpole Street house, seemed willing to have me around, or to join them with a girl in the evenings, and I saw quite a lot of them that winter.

Granny Gertrude, never comfortably off, had devoted her life to working for charity; she doted on my father and could see a physical resemblance in me. Together we experienced the shattering crash of a V2 rocket landing at Marble Arch and we sat in a friend's debenture seats to hear oratorio at the Albert Hall. Strangely in one who must have been brought up in almost rural surroundings at Rigby, Gertrude (who died two years later) was a deep-dyed town's person. In late middle age she had been staying with a friend in the country and was taken, apparently for the first time, to see cows being milked. "Quite disgusting," she told my astonished mother afterwards, "I had absolutely *no* idea our milk came like that!"

On Germany's surrender a weight (cliché though it sounds) seemed truly to lift from one's mind. On VE Day I joined a cheerful, waving crowd outside the Palace as the King and Queen appeared several times on the balcony. During an unusually long interval a voice behind me called "Come on George, leave the washing up till afterwards!" At last certified as fit, I was told to report to Supreme Headquarters Allied Expeditionary Forces (SHAEF) at Versailles. Arriving at the Park West flat to say goodbye I found my mother, just back in England, being removed to hospital by ambulance. Terrified that she might be dangerously ill, I had a really miserable journey until a call from Paris revealed it was pneumonia. With penicillin now available it was not serious.

Next day three Lysander spotter aircraft flew southeast, low over eastern France, two army clerks and I each in solitary state behind a pilot. Refuelling at Nancy, we landed at the Oberwiesenfeld airport, Munich, peace just three days old. Our section of SHAEF intelligence would look for documents or the personnel of German ministries lurking down in Bavaria. Housed to the south of the city in an American mess, and deep in the American zone of Germany, my diary soon grumbles about unpalatable food – jam spewing across eggs and toast on the breakfast platter, hash for most meals and at lunchtime "nasty cold tea". 'Liberating' was the current euphemism for looting, then much in vogue. Our mess had just liberated quantities of white wine and too much soon gave me colitis. In Munich's devastated city centre great cliffs of rubble had been bulldozed aside to make way for traffic. The Pfeiffer's flat had disappeared, and exploring in streets around the (lightly damaged) Rathaus, where I had so often walked and bicycled, I several times lost my way.

Most of the Americans with whom we messed seemed even at this very early stage to want the strict rules against fraternising with Germans relaxed. Despite all I knew to the contrary, no local Germans to whom I talked (illicitly) would own up to having supported the Nazis. "We all knew the war was lost two years ago", "they should never have fought for Berlin", "the party members....". I knew it was almost impossible to have openly opposed the Nazis, but I wanted to hear them be sorry for having started this gruesome war – not just sorry for having lost it. That they did not, and that many Germans were overly unctuous towards their conquerors, stuck in my craw for years.

Across the border in Austria, French troops had now taken over from the Americans and with typical Gallic contrariness promptly lifted the ban on fraternisation. Houses in Innsbruck were bedecked with Austrian and Tyrolean flags, road signs offered a 'cordiale bienvenue dans le Tyrol'. With a Wellington contemporary I spent a weekend motoring around, and we stayed at the flat my companion had rented pre-war. The French were very hospitable, their troops thin on the ground, a company in place where the Americans would have put a battalion. Lunching in a restaurant with two Austrians they confirmed that their new occupiers were inconspicuous, polite and indeed quite welcome. But life was not easy. The younger, a student, said his ration card for eleven days usually lasted for three; after that he subsisted on unrationed soup or begged for milk. On the way back to Munich we stopped in Oberammagau to speak to two bearded characters who had acted in

73

the four-yearly Passion Play. One said he had been Judas Iscariot, the other Nathaniel; aged eighty-one, he claimed he had acted in every play since 1880. We asked after Jesus but were told he was in police custody.

At Potsdam the allied heads of state had just agreed that all territory captured by the advancing Americans in Thuringia must be handed over to the Russians. By an odd coincidence Geoffrey Barton, fresh from the staff college at Quetta in India, was in an organisation rather similar to mine just down the road at Starnberg. He had just been told to take a German staff officer, now a prisoner, to find and retrieve some top-secret documents the Germans had buried near Jena before the incoming Russians could find them. Geoffrey, a major, asked if I might accompany him as interpreter, and rather surprisingly this was agreed.

Late in June, armed with intelligence passes from the American Sixth and Seventh Armies, my brother-in-law and I set off in an open staff car accompanied by Oberst-Leutnant Euler, lately of the Foreign Armies section of the Oberkommando West, and the colonel's guard, Private McCallum of the Black Watch, who sat with him in front as driver. Sticking to the 'no-frat' rule soon proved unworkable, so Geoffrey asked the Colonel for his parole and on the road the four of us ate and drank together. Country roads in Germany were in poor shape, long neglected for the autobahns, and it was a second day before we left the pastel coloured walls and pointed spires of Bavaria for darker, timber-framed houses and onion domes as we neared Thuringia.

Our hosts at Ohrsdruf on the provincial border were a detachment of American counter-intelligence operatives. Living grandly in a hideously vulgar pseudo-castle complete with copper roof and bogus coats of arms recently built by a Nazi, the ten or so agents of the detachment were very hospitable, laid back and excellent company. All bi-lingual, they seemed quite ruthless in their job, claiming cheerfully that forty-five suicides had so far resulted from their interrogations. I sat in on one session while an agent systematically probed the stories of two German youths. Suspecting they belonged to the Werewolves, an organisation of fanatical former members of the Hitler Jugend then dedicated to sabotaging the invaders, he deliberately and histrionically scared them witless. Finally both broke down. For me it was an impressive but uncomfortable performance. Our hosts told us that rumours of the allies attacking the Russians, which had been started by the German underground, had been widely believed in the French zone. The local German population was now terrified at the prospect of Russian occupation, but there was no sign as yet that Russian troops were on the move.

Armed with our intelligence passes, Geoffrey and I set out next day on what we called a recce, but more honestly was a swan, to check this out. We found the Americans had indeed been pulling their troops back westwards with all speed, even using both tracks of the east-west autobahn. At Jena, where we had rather hoped to acquire some field glasses, inhabitants said all had long since been bought up, sometimes, we were told, at prices higher than pre-war. Elsewhere the hilly wooded countryside seemed totally deserted.

When the four of us returned that afternoon, we had reached the middle of a great pine forest in the Georgenthal when Colonel Euler called out for the car to stop. Leading us a hundred yards off the road, he began to measure distances between the tall tree trunks and finally indicated a spot. At three feet into the forest earth Pte

McCallum's spade hit something hard: cautious scraping revealed the curved top of a sizeable metal trunk. Though Euler had assured us there were no booby traps, Geoffrey sensibly handed him the spade. We stood back as he took off his long leather overcoat, and with the trunk finally out, opened it up. All was well – it contained only papers and files. Two others, Euler said, were somewhere close by. An hour later, after much pacing around and some abortive digging, we had found nothing more. Geoffrey decided we must return to Ohrsdruf before the dusk curfew made us overly conspicuous. We hoped to return next day.

Back at the castle, the Counter-Intelligence Corps was already packing up. The Russians were on the way, they said, and advised us to be off bright and early. At dawn next morning we had driven only a mile when, rounding a bend, our car ran over a layer of broken glass laid presumably by the Werewolves. Two rear tyres punctured. Repair kits were like gold dust in those days. Although we eventually located another spare tyre back in Ohrsdruf, we were still fitting it when, to our considerable alarm, the Russians came in sight. Shambling along the verges of the main road that ran parallel half a mile away we could see long lines of scruffy-looking solders. Others moved like beaters up the adjoining fields. Lumbering down the road itself came a motley collection of wagons and handcarts. Most of the vehicles were ox-drawn, one which particularly appealed to Geoffrey had a bullock yoked on one side and a donkey on the other. Nothing in this primitive convoy seemed to be mechanised; the cavalcade looked for all the world like Wellington's baggage train lumbering across the plains of Spain.

Our best bet now seemed to be to hurry down side roads until we were ahead of the column, then head for the new zonal boundary at Eisenach. There we approached the border very cautiously, but to our dismay saw that a Russian sentry was already in place. To arrive in a German-made staff car with a German Colonel in uniform did not seem at all a good idea. After a brief discussion Colonel Euler put on Private McCallum's greatcoat and took the wheel; McCallum put on mine and joined us British officers on the back seat. Thus rearranged we drove up a lot more confidently than we felt. Neither side of course could understand the other. However, after Geoffrey had rather expertly, if regretfully, parted with a bottle of Guerlain perfume intended for Geraldine, the sentry raised no objection and let us through.

Next day we deposited our contribution to the military history of the Second World War in the enormous I.G. Farben building at Frankfurt, which had miraculously escaped torrential bombing and now housed the US headquarters in Europe (ETOUSA). We had both taken a shine to Colonel Euler. As we drove him back to internment I asked his professional opinion of the allied armies. He sounded genuinely scared of the Russian menace, but said that in the High Command they had rated one British or American division the equal of two Russian. He considered Patton and Monty had been our best allied generals, but added that he thought British army tactics had been too inflexible.

Soon after this I was transferred to the British zone to await my next posting from London. Headquarters, 21st Army Group at Bad Oeynhausen sent me to convert a grand *Schloss* and shooting estate, until recently owned by Goering, into a military government leave centre. Predictably I was introduced at Hanover as "our new S.O. III (Huntin', Shootin' and Fishin')." Springe, where the estate was, and some local towns like Hameln of Pied Piper fame, and

Pyrmont, where typhus and polio were raging, were undamaged. However, anything to renovate a building, especially skilled labour, took considerable scrounging. The driver of my small Ford, a very blond 22 year old, had been in the Hitler Jugend and served with the Luftwaffe in the Crimea. Fascinated by new technology, his current ambition was to join the RAF and fight the Japanese. This unlikely scenario was soon frustrated by the announcement of VJ Day. Oddly all German shops were ordered to close for this occasion, although whether their proprietors were supposed to laugh or to cry was not explained.

Long before this job could be completed I had to report back to Army Group headquarters, was promoted to major and posted to the staff of the Economic Adviser to the Commander, 8 Corps, stationed at Ploen in Schleswig-Holstein.

My boss for the next six months would be a civilian, a Mr Dennison-Ross, with a lieutenant-colonel, another major and an English secretary on his Control Commission staff. If it sounds daft for this middle-aged economist to be lumbered with a young soldier who knew nothing of economics or commerce and had never set foot in a factory or town hall, the government of Germany in that first winter of peace was entirely dominated by the army, everything being done by or through it. It did not need an expert to see Germany's economic plight – it hit you in the face. In the province's largest town, Kiel, only one house in twelve was undamaged. The basic daily ration, further reduced in February to only 1,050 calories, amounted to little more than starvation. Fortunately Schleswig-Holstein was largely an agricultural province, but most people were aware of the eight million refugees countrywide, now entitled 'displaced persons', who urgently needed food and housing. One rarely saw a German lorry on the roads, yet coal at the pithead or peat for fuel could not be distributed without them.

These at any rate were the crucial topics for Oberpraesident Stelzer of Schleswig-Holstein, Burgermaster Petersen of Hamburg and assorted experts on the *Wirtschaftstrat Nord*, the economic committee that became my particular baby. It was (thank goodness) the Germans who had to take the decisions; whatever advice ADR gave the Corps Commander was not for me to worry about. Meanwhile the villa we lived in was comfortable, Schleswig-Holstein the most beautiful and most English part of Germany I had yet seen, and Ploen, isolated by a string of small lakes, a charming, undamaged market town.

In Cornwall at the end of October I was reunited with Antony, who was staying with our parents. Although chrome yellow from anti-malarial Mepacrin, he looked astonishingly fit after the long recuperative sea voyage home. Neither then nor later did he want to talk about his three and a half years' experience of Jap barbarity and their pitiless treatment of POW's on that heinous Burma railway line. On board ship he had written a sober account, which we all read avidly. Much later I heard that he personally had been mentioned in despatches for his conduct as a prisoner. What splendid character he must have displayed in those circumstances!

My father was on retirement leave. In 1942 he had commanded the land forces that moved down from Diego Suarez on the northern tip of Madagascar to capture the capital, Tananarivo, from the Vichy French. After General le Gentilhomme had taken over as Free French Governor-General of Madagascar, my father remained commanding the East African troops there, the distant islands of the Seychelles, Réunion and Mauritius, and flying dangerously between them across thousands of miles of ocean. Early in 1945 he was released from this backwater to head a British Military Mission to Greece. British troops occupying Athens on the heels of the retreating Germans had themselves been attacked in strength by communist-led Greek partisans who, with the Germans ousted, were now determined to seize power. Most of the world's press was inclined to regard the E.L.A.S. partisans favourably as Greek patriots. Churchill, however, foresaw in Greece the likelihood of a communist take-over such as soon befell Czechoslovakia, and he flew to Athens on Boxing Day 1944 to sort things out. The partisans were forced to withdraw. While the King of Greece waited in the wings until a plebiscite should vote in favour of his return, Archbishop Damaskinos was installed as Regent; democratic elections were to be held in due course.

It was into this highly charged situation that my father arrived. The language of diplomacy was again French and his position politically sensitive. For some months he apparently did well. Then the Greek government, having re-organised its army, decided to appoint a lieutenant-general to command and requested, for the sake of appearances, that my father be promoted to the same rank. He was called to London. Sir Alan Brooke, the C.I.G.S., insisted that he had several younger Lieutenant-Generals previously commanding corps who needed appointments. By ill luck my father had been refused this promotion and probable knighthood in spite of his protests, and he had requested permission to retire. As a sop he was given six months' leave on full pay, which he was now enjoying. To my knowledge he never spoke of the matter again.

At Christmas 1945, having wangled a duty pass from A.D.R. to visit the Danish Ministry of Food over a long weekend, I was driven through that neat and orderly country by an army friend. In Copenhagen the English in uniform were highly popular. Well-dressed girls smiled at us in cheerfully decorated streets and all the shops looked amazingly well stocked. After the gloom and grey of Germany the atmosphere in Copenhagen was like a shaft of sunlight. The Hoeg family and their two daughters shared with us their Christmas Eve, the Danes' big day, took us to church on Christmas Day, and on Boxing Day to lunch at the Hotel d'Angleterre. Breakfast at our own hotel cost 7/6d, which we thought expensive, but food seemed surprisingly plentiful and at the Angleterre four of us ate our way through twenty-three large smorrebrod, each the equivalent of a course.

Through the Hoegs I met a slim, shy eighteen-year-old with long dark hair, whom I found very attractive. Unlike most of the Danes, Ruth spoke little English, but when I suggested 'deutsch?' she shook her head angrily. I asked her out to dance. Sitting out she finally relaxed a little and told me in fair German that her parents had been active in the resistance. Last year they had all been arrested. Her mother had been sent to a concentration camp, Belsen I think, from which she had never returned. Ruth herself had been intended for Neuengamme, but thanks to a Dane serving in the SS she had escaped and spent the last months of the war in hiding with the underground. Much upset by now and almost in tears, she began to inveigh against the Germans.

I had never met anyone directly involved in the resistance and certainly never before encountered such virulent hatred. How, she kept demanding, could we British be so *lenient* with such

81

barbarians? After eight months the ban against fraternising with Germans was still strongly supported by many serving in military government – often, I noticed, by those who spoke no German. Personally I had broken the taboo only once. Together with a colleague we had called on a university professor at Kiel living with his family in two cramped rooms in a cellar. My diary noted 'it is almost impossible to find a safe subject'. As the evening in Copenhagen went on I realised one cannot absorb hatred at second hand. All I could really feel for Ruth was pity, and a great sadness that one so young (and, of course, pretty) should harbour so much bitterness.

Scarcely anyone in the Occupying Power at this time was ever beholden to Germans, and this makes my friend Ian Sconce's story worth telling. At the end of August 1939, Ian had been at Marburg University for two years studying for a PhD. He handed in his thesis and, with only oral exams still to come, was warned by our consulate to leave the country immediately. By good luck finding a solitary petrol pump still in use on an isolated road, he filled his car and in due course reached Switzerland. In May 1945 Ian was, like me, flown back into Germany from Paris and, circling to land on a temporary airstrip north of Frankfurt, found himself peering from the side window of the Dakota at that identical petrol pump.

Posted as a German speaker to the Allied Control Council's secretariat in shattered Berlin, Ian managed to contact his former professor, who with considerable difficulty located his original thesis. With the connivance of the Control Commission's print room, the necessary copies were printed and subsequently accepted. An enlightened management then gave Ian permission to travel to Marburg. There, as a British officer in uniform, he was quizzed at interview by the pariahs of Europe. This rare and civilising moment ended happily with the award of his doctorate.

Back at Ploen, though I liked my boss, ADR, and got on well with the others in our small mess, I was beginning to feel unsettled. Ignorance of matters economic confined me to secretarial work on the parochial *Wirtschaftstrat Nord*, whereas any real power lay with the Economic Board for the British zone as a whole. Germany was already two distinct countries. When two 'communist' Germans from Schwerin, just across our border with Mecklenburg, came to a meeting in Lubeck, I noticed they were treated by their fellow Germans with deferential suspicion like medieval ambassadors from a potentially dangerous neighbour.

Demob was now in full swing. Michael Pocock, with me on a second visit to Copenhagen, said he would be off soon to join Shell Company in Venezuela. Twenty-five years later we met again in London. By then he was the head of all Royal Dutch Shell, by far the ablest man I have ever known well. Rumours were circulating about gloomy prospects in the post-war army. Personally I was not keen to return to regimental duty. Since neither battalion of the Fifth was in Europe, under the heinous new 'group' system I might find myself shunted into any northern county regiment that happened to be in Germany. Indeed, I was beginning to wonder whether there was really much point in staying in the army. Why spend your life training for something you sincerely hope will never happen again?

My parents' original intention had been to retire to the Georgian stone house with its stabling and forty acres they had bought at Charlton, near Banbury, in 1938, and there continue to hunt. Confronted by the austere and very different conditions of life in England eight years later, my father changed his mind. On leave with Didi in the early spring of 1946, I found that my parents had already gone back to Kenya. Antony, all shoulder muscles from his work on the Burma railway, would soon be joining Shell Company, which had treated its employees particularly well whilst they were prisoners of war.

Fired by Harold Nicholson's books and articles in *The Spectator* about the newly merged diplomatic and consular services, renamed the Foreign Service, I was beginning to harbour unlikely aspirations in that direction. First I must get to Berlin where things really happened. Divisions of the Control Commission corresponded roughly to the functions of national government: hence the Political division, which handled external affairs and employed several members of the Foreign Service, looked the one to aim for.

A kindly man, ADR agreed I go to Berlin and try my luck. Margaret, his thirty-ish secretary, who had been recognised in the office to have a (totally bewildering) crush on me, asked to come along too 'to see Berlin'; we drove off together in the Auto Union saloon that six months' possession had already made 'mine'. Headquarters of Military Government in Minden said the only vacancy in the Political division had already gone to a candidate for the Foreign Service; however, as there was a possibility of a job in the Army division, we continued to the zonal checkpoint at Helmstedt, then up the Allies' almost deserted autobahn through the Russian zone to Berlin.

"You would be our representative at the *Wast*", a colonel told me in the miraculously undamaged modern office block that housed CCG headquarters. Even a job in something so utterly dismal as an army records office *(Wehrmachtsauskunftstelle)* had to be less ignominious than returning jobless with Margaret to Ploen. "All the German army records are held in the American sector on about thirty million cards and forms. German staff are working flat out under tripartite supervision – no Russians – to reduce their huge backlog in sending out death notices. They cannot finish before the autumn. Of course," the Colonel went on "from a humanitarian standpoint that is very important, but the *Wast* holds among other things a nominal roll of the German army by units – its Order of Battle. The Russians maintain this could be used to mobilise an army in the future and are insisting it be broken up. So the Allied Co-ordinating Committee has ruled that the *Wast* must stop work on the 1st June. Its records will be divided between the Americans, the French and ourselves. Your job", he added "is to tell us what, if anything, we should take over."

Relieved that it would be only for six weeks, and with a chance to scout around, I moved into the CCG mess in the Grunewald, reporting next morning at a complex of makeshift wooden huts near the sector boundary. The American lieutenant-colonel in charge introduced me to his staff – a French major and captain, and a captain and two subalterns from the U.S. – then gave me carte-blanche. Looking around the buildings it was soon clear I could barely understand the wording of the forms, let alone make sense of the Germans' intricate system for recording casualties and POWs. Fortunately for me both the junior American officers spoke near-perfect German, knew the organisation in detail and oversaw the daily despatch of hundreds of death notices. Both were appalled at the prospect of such early closure: tens of thousands of German families would suffer. Impressed, I spoke to the Colonel, who made

85

it clear he had a job to do by the first of June and was not to be sidetracked. The French were totally blinkered: their only interest was in intelligence about war criminals, collaborators and anyone who had committed crimes in France.

By now really emotionally involved for the first time, I drove down to the zone to report to 'A' branch of 21 Army Group. The Assistant Adjutant-General in charge of German affairs, immediately sympathetic, agreed we recommend his brigadier ask the Co-ordinating Committee to postpone closure for despatch of death notices until the end of the year. "But", he added "we may not get much help."

Sure enough his boss was paunchy and loud mouthed "Not our bloody pigeon", the brigadier said immediately, "We'll bid for the POW records. They'll tell us about our own people. Death notices aren't the army's business – entirely up to the CCG. They'll get the flack anyway." With considerable difficulty we persuaded him to have a word 'higher up'.

West Berlin looked surprisingly beautiful. Hundreds of chestnut trees and lilacs were in bloom on the suburban avenues of the Grunewald. Elsewhere flowering window boxes perched in the windows of bombed houses, along with the leaves of shrubs and surviving trees, hid much of the damage. You could move freely between national sectors. There was considerably more fratting here than down in the British zone, especially in the American sector; I sensed however, that the inhabitants were less well disposed. Comparatively respectable frat spots in our sector, like the Royal on the Kurfuerstendamm and the more tawdry Femina, were described as 'night clubs' but obliged to close at 10.00 pm. They sold ruinously expensive food bought only by Germans, provided a dance floor and music, and bottles of champagne that could be obtained through the waiter for twenty cigarettes. Most fratting, of course, had only one objective. Sitting in the cinema I watched the hero follow his girl out into a paddock. An American voice beside me piped up, "Hey buddy, don't forget your bar of chocolate." British troops in Berlin wore a black flash in a red circle on their uniforms, variously interpreted as 'British troops surrounded by the Red Army' or 'Demob surrounded by red tape'.

Monty was rumoured to be left wing and to have (unpopular) ideas about democratising relations between officers and other ranks. He had just left to become the new CIGS. In the top executive body, the Allied Co-ordinating Committee, an American member of their secretariat told me that Generals Robertson and Clay, and to a lesser extent the French General Koeltz, got along well, but the new Russian, Dratvin, was both unintelligent and obstructive. "The Russians always approach problems from a devious angle", he said. "They allow long and apparently fruitful discussions before reverting unerringly to their original standpoint – wildly frustrating.".Koeltz frequently disagreed with the Americans and British, but was under close control from the French government. The atmosphere at meetings was often extremely tense.

After a fortnight of no decision about the death notices I did not know whom to tackle. Bursting into the outer office of a major-general, I was aborted by his staff without getting to see him. Then General Clay suddenly decided the Americans after all wanted a share in the counter-intelligence records. The *Wast* closed – how much was burned I never knew.

Life, so the story goes, is like a game of bar billiards. In your twenties you can slosh around and score freely, but at forty the bar drops and from then on you must play with the assets you have left. Sloshing around I missed a job in the Allied Secretariat to a Russian speaker but scored at the British Secretariat. When 1st June arrived I was already employed by the Control Commission at Berlin's Lancaster House and being fed the 'larger picture'. From the minutes of the Allied Control Council (where Monty had been no great shakes) I could see what a pain the Russians were being – also how, for example, the French had frustrated a vital agreement made at Potsdam to treat Germany as one economic unit. It was clear that much had to be sacrificed to reach compromises. Nevertheless it seemed to me then (and it still does) that to stop the Germans from completing the despatch of death notices to wives and families was unnecessarily barbarous.

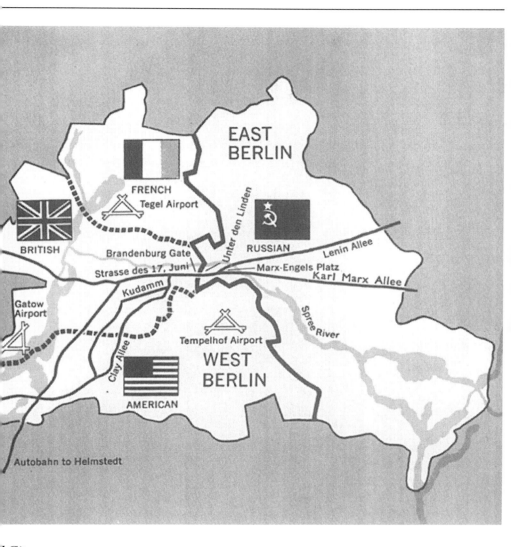

EAST
BERLIN

FRENCH
Tegel Airport

Unter den Linden

RUSSIAN

Lenin Allee

BRITISH

Brandenburg Gate

Strasse des 17. Juni

Marx-Engels Platz

Karl Marx Allee

Kudamm

Gatow
Airport

Clay Allee

Spree River

Tempelhof Airport

WEST
BERLIN

AMERICAN

Autobahn to Helmstedt

City

CHAPTER SIX

HERE IN Berlin we are BERCOMB and our bosses at Norfolk House, London are CONFOLK. Germany is hot news and down the corridor from my office F.O. telegrams in code or clear stream continuously through the communications room. The Chief Secretary is a brigadier. I am allocated to 'G' (for Governmental) section, led by a naval lieutenant-commander (E), which deals with the Political, Public Relations and Information Service Control and Legal divisions of the Control Commission. The job is pretty well exactly what I wanted.

At my first big meeting, J.B. Hynd, small dark and bald with a Scottish accent, a Labour politician and our new political master, sits opposite a thickset, heavy man in RAF uniform. I note that the new Military Governor, Sir Sholto Douglas, does not call him 'Sir'. In terms of my favourite board game, 'L'attaque', a Marshal of the RAF presumably equals a Chancellor of the Duchy of Lancaster. Everyone on the London team ('We run this show, don't forget') is a civilian; most of those on the Berlin side, except the Military Governor's 'political adviser with ambassador status', Sir William Strang, are soldiers ('We do the job, and we are the ones with the answers'). A very wide-ranging and often detailed discussion of the situation follows; the atmosphere improves slowly from cold to lukewarm. Helping in this, never ruffled, brilliantly clear-minded and always well-informed is the Deputy Military Governor, Lieutenant-General Sir Brian (later Lord) Robertson, son of the extraordinary individual who rose from footman and private soldier to become a Field Marshal and Chief of the Imperial General Staff during the First World War. Polite but always decisive, the D.M.G. sums up the outcome of a contentious point and turns to Hynd "So you want us to do..... so-and-so, Sir? You do? Right – it will be done." We move to the next item.

In addition to preparing minutes, my section does some work for the D.M.G., who has his own Military Assistant, and for the Deputy Chief of Staff (Policy), a major-general. While I am waiting in the M.A.'s office, youngish Mr Bellenger, newly elected M.P. saunters in with a snide comment about the size of the offices. He is only Financial Secretary to the War Office and the D.C.O. (Policy), General Erskine, greets him with, to my mind, overmuch warmth. I write in my diary 'eighteen months ago *that* was only a staff captain 'Q'!'

Quickly loaded with sufficient work I soon met more people, and my social life improved. In addition to frequent drinks parties there were the usual expatriate club activities – tennis or drinks around the pool at the Blau Weiss officers' club in the Grunewald. The Four Hundred, a social club only, was more polyglot ('You spik English?'.'A few – and you?' 'Many'). Fuel and maintenance for my illicit car were freely available and there was dinghy sailing out at Gatow most weekends. In the shattered centre of the Soviet sector, where even by day the empty streets retained their eerie atmosphere of rape and menace, I went to several performances of grand opera and, unforgettably, heard Yehudi Menuhin in Berlin playing the Beethoven violin concerto.

Rumours were always circulating about looted Mercedes being shipped by devious routes back to England, or how millions of marks acquired on the black market had somehow been laundered on the Paris bourse. For a while many such stories will have been well-founded. I am sure most of us were venal, though the great majority were doubtless, like me, timid, wanting only to exchange goods bought cheaply through the NAAFI or American PX for larger amounts of marks. 'BAFs' (British Armed Forces Special Vouchers), when introduced in August that year as our local currency, came as a tiresome obstacle to living free. Soon afterwards the entire staff at Lancaster House was summoned for a lucid survey of present policies from General Robertson – 'nothing' I noted grandly 'new to me' – and given a well-disguised pep talk about our dubious behaviour. "Such a good 'extemper' speech", Miss H of the registry called it afterwards.

Events in Germany, as we observed them happening or followed in telegrams, seemed to us at the time vitally important, the very warp of history. Under a quadripartite agreement many thousands of Germans were being evicted by train from newly occupied Polish Silesia into the British zone, where of course there was an acute shortage of housing as well as of food. Telegrams began to fly to and fro from London about restricting this flow of DPs unilaterally (for good and sufficient reasons I need not go into) to two trains a week, using British troops to enforce compliance. I began to wonder what mayhem would result. (Nothing very serious, in fact, did.). When death sentences were passed at the Nuremberg trial on Field Marshal Keitel and Hitler's military adviser, General Jodl, both asked to be shot rather than hanged. The

Control Council argued over this and one or two other issues for eight hours, the Russians as usual saying 'niet'. In the end Sholto Douglas cabled CONFOLK for Ernest Bevin, "It is a matter for your conscience." They were hanged. Enjoying this new vantage point, and emboldened by seeing actual diplomats at work, I decided to have a shot at joining the Foreign Service myself.

In Kenya, captivated by the magnificent panorama from a hillside a hundred miles northwest of Nairobi, my father had bought his Shangri La. When my mother arrived in the spring she was driven up immediately to see it. The rains, she told me later, had just started. From bleak and windswept grasslands at eight thousand feet they turned downhill from the slippery murram main road, then over a narrow tree-trunk bridge across the fast flowing Oraimutia. Taking a dash at the opposite hillside they spun to a halt half way up its steep, rock strewn surface. Eventually pushed up by passing Africans, their car bellied more than once in climbing the rutted access road. Finally they reached a dark, dripping avenue of close-planted fir trees, soon to be christened 'Cold lairs'. On an expanse of Kikuyu grass at the end stood a smallish, rectangular wooden bungalow and a few native huts. Farm-built from offcuts covered with cedar bark, my mother's new home had a palm-thatched roof, also dripping, no electric light, no telephone, and no running water. Outside, under the lowering skies at that moment, there was no view. She sat in the car and wept.

"Gerald wants to be on the spot when they start building", my mother began to enthuse in weekly airmails from Barry's Hotel at Thomson's Falls, "the house plans are entirely his." Longing to be back in Kenya to see what they were doing, I had by the autumn become due some leave. "How would you get out there?" my brigadier asked. The war being only recently over, all of central Europe from Kiel to Palermo was still under military rule; Nairobi seemed a good deal more remote than it does today. "Mostly hop lifts, Sir, I hope." A reply which seemed to tickle the Chief Secretary. Anyway, he agreed to let me try.

On the evening of 23 October 1946, armed with a travel warrant for an 'appointment' in Frankfurt, I caught the U.S. Berliner express from the American sector. After 'real scrambled eggs' for breakfast and a fresh set of travel documents, I continued next afternoon in a re-upholstered, grey painted Dakota owned by the British European Aircraft Corporation, to Vienna, like Berlin under quadripartite rule. A fellow passenger from the Ministry for Supply, also staying at the Park Hotel, kindly asked me to join his largish party for dinner that evening. Sensing a good moment afterwards I broached the question of getting to Nairobi, for which my plans included cadging further air transport, first down to Rome and from there, hopefully, on to Cairo. Several people had suggestions. In the corridor afterwards a fairly senior air force officer drew me aside. He was, he said, Chief Air Traffic Officer at R.A.F. headquarters in Udine, northern Italy. He had heard our conversation. If he could offer me a friendly word of advice – *"forget it"*.

Vienna next day proved to be damaged only on the scale of London rather than Berlin. Neither over lunch at the Officers' Club in the Kinski Palace, nor afterwards at the travel bureau, housed equally grandly in the Palace at Schoenbrunn, could I find a soul going down to Italy. There seemed nothing for it but to catch the sleeper that evening as far as Villach in southern Austria; trains at that time went no further.

Over breakfast in the Hotel Post at Villach I was joined by an American official from the Allied Commission, also trying to head south. Carrying our bags, we walked out of the town and soon managed to hitch a lorry to the frontier. After sitting for a dismal hour on our luggage, a passing army fifteen hundredweight from the Argylls then swept us through splendid scenery over to Udine. I approached the airport nervously: all flights to Rome had been suspended because of the weather. For the first time I would have to fork out for a rail ticket. At 2.10 am next morning an impressive looking steam monster, hissing and clanking and pretentiously called 'The International' pulled in at Udine. The first post-war Calais to Naples express carried neither sleepers nor any food, she shuffled slowly along on bad stretches, speeded up, stopped again. Breakfast was taken on the platform at Verona, lunch at Bologna and an early supper in Florence. Twenty-seven hours later, at 5.15 am in the morning of 27 October, we finally reached Rome.

According to my optimistic schedule I was due next day in Cairo. Sure enough, at Ciampino airfield later that morning the pilot of a Lancaster freighter promised me a lift to Cairo (Almaza). Installed in high glee now at the Continental Hotel, I took off for some sightseeing. On the square outside St Peter's a crowd was assembling for a Beatification. Inside the Cathedral's main doorway thousands of people were moving around the vast interior, a brass band playing in the gallery above. Once inside I was shocked by the loud chatter and laughter, behaviour more suited, I thought, to the foyer of a theatre. Suddenly trumpets blared and hundreds of cluster lights blazed spectacularly in the transept, conversations stopped, there was some clapping. Through the crowd to my right came soldiers in black pantaloons sporting what looked like Spanish medieval helmets, and after them four dignitaries, all in black with white ruff collars and wearing long gold chains. As they passed between lines of black and scarlet papal guards there were shouts of 'Viva il Papa!' The narrow head of Pius XII appeared: a sharp ascetic face, prim gold specs, he was carried on a tapestried throne by eight boys and richly robed as in a portrait by Titian. I thought he looked both scholar and bigot. Behind him were the vivid cloaks of the cardinals, more soldiers. Chattering resumed as the procession moved on up the thronged main aisle. There was a short service, some indifferent singing, and the panoply returned, again to great theatre. I was impressed.

Before 7.00 am next morning my suitcase was already in the aircraft at Ciampino airfield and I was having a cup of tea before take-off when the resident traffic officer appeared. "Totally unauthorised" he said, brooking no argument, "take it out – you can't travel." On the other side of the airfield all the T.W.A. pilots were for some reason on strike. Back in Rome I was told that every military air passage had now to be referred to G.H.Q. Padua; this entailed, inter alia, at least three days delay. B.O.A.C. had not a seat to Cairo for six days, nor any of the other airlines for ten. In desperation I booked with an Italian company as far as Athens – the flight was cancelled. Eventually it seemed best to take our embassy's advice and go by train down to Sicily. There was a chance of a place on B.O.A.C.'s Southampton-Cairo flying boat, which paused there to refuel.

After a night out I turned up late for the 0620 express to Naples and missed it. The next train would be a slow, one-class, non-corridor electric. Arriving now in service dress in good time, I spotted some space in an already very crowded compartment and climbed in. Immediately the carriage went completely silent. From both long benches, rows of Italian peasants and their families stared with unwinking intensity at this young foreign officer, slowly taking in his new medal ribbons, his polished buttons and Sam Browne belt. The war was very recent. Politely they made space for me at a window, and watched like a fish in a tank. I heaved my luggage on to the rack as the train pulled out and stared fixedly out of the window.

Five minutes later, without any warning, my suitcase fell with a thump into my lap. Getting up to put it back and clutching the case my mackintosh fell over my head. There were suppressed giggles from two small boys on the bench opposite. I put the case down in the central aisle for safety, unfortunately snapping off the handle of someone's umbrella. In the absence of any Italian it seemed better not to notice.

Some time later I had more or less regained my composure when the train stopped at a country halt. Out in the sunshine vendors were calling their wares. Winding down the narrow top section of the window to buy some grapes, I squeezed my head through it, fumbling meanwhile in my pocket. Several coins spilled and I had to scrabble for them on the floor. Back again, I had grapes in one hand and was just passing cash through the window with the other when the guard whistled. The train started, my head jerked up and my nose banged down smartly on the window surround. Blood gushed freely. Immediately half my fellow passengers were on their feet. From a babble of solicitude and incomprehensible advice I remember someone offering me a phial of smelling salts. A handkerchief to my importunate nose and waving away help, I could only smile and nod from my corner, more embarrassed than I ever remember.

Hours later, as our train stopped frequently to let others pass, we rumbled along the sea shore past chalk cliffs split by gullies of short scrub, dawdling at little, yellow-and-white walled towns, where the locals came out to chat in the sunshine. At the Oriente, the Services' transit hotel in Naples, there was a power failure and no water. Then another ten hours in the train via Messina finally landed me at the B.O.A.C.'s Rest House in Augusta, a straggling, east coast port much used after the invasion of Sicily.

Next day the twenty-two seater flying boat came through. For the first time in weeks, they said, it was full. Soon cursing myself for having left Rome, I was followed around the streets of fecund Augusta by swarms of highly commercial youths calling 'Hi Joe!' and sometimes 'Jig-a-jig?' There was one fleapit cinema and a smelly sea. Again the next day the flying boat was full, and on the one after, over-weight. At long last, acquiring an armchair from a luckless passenger who had been disembarked with a ruptured eardrum, I watched the bow wave surge excitingly past the window of our little six-seater cabin at take-off. Stairs led up to a pink bar-cum-galley and there were two blue-painted lavatories. The Short Sunderland was not unduly noisy and extremely comfortable, but so slow that it was dusk, six and a half hours later, before we splashed into the darkening Nile at Cairo.

David Scott, clever elder son of the Scotts at Wellington, was Chief Radar Officer at the still-extant Military Mission. Time was now really pressing as I had committed myself to sit the Foreign Service exam four days hence in Nairobi. After a quick telephone call, a taxi took me through the frenzied racket of Cairene car horns to David and Vera's flat out at Heliopolis. Next morning, with help from David and a priority passage from GHQ, more than a month's pay secured the last seat on the Cairo-Nairobi Dakota service.

Flying in the days before the high altitude jet still retained vestiges of romance, of covering vast distances and voyaging across foreign lands. Although our converted Dakota was unpressurised its canvas bucket seats were more comfortable than they looked. After an inapposite brunch of eggs and bacon on a sweltering airstrip at Wadi Halfa, we flew on down the river. Black sentries outside our bedrooms in the RAF mess at Khartoum wore the high khaki turbans and sharply pressed apron shirts of the Sudan Defence Force. Like most of us I was driven that evening into central Khartoum along broad tree-lined avenues of impeccable colonial bungalows, each with its own veranda, and dined overlooking the Nile at the Grand Hotel.

Take-off was in the cool of morning at 6.00 am. For some time the bright silver lines of innumerable irrigation ditches intersected the green of cultivation. We droned on at 6,000 feet over vast dun plains of grass and the green and brown of flat-topped acacias. Stopping on a grass airfield at Marakal to refuel, the company's airfield employees hurried out with the steps, all stark naked to a man. Passengers were ushered into a grass-thatched shed and fed a second breakfast. After a hotel lunch in the heat of Juba the Dakota climbed to 11,000 feet, crossed a corner of Lake Victoria, refuelled again at Kisumu, then lurched over the Kenya highlands and, nine hours from Khartoum, landed in Nairobi. It was 6.00 pm on Armistice Day 1946, exactly three weeks after I had left Berlin.

Installed at the Muthaiga Club I sat my exam two days later. My nostalgia for Kenya came mainly from wartime memories of the Northern Frontier District, of walking in the bush in the sparkle of early morning. As the sun rose little white clouds formed like rumpled sheets along the wide horizon, then slowly towered and billowed. I remembered the sensation of boundless space, of moving in a timeless, natural world that can hardly have changed since man first began to walk upright. Now, with the war over, Kenya would be something quite different. Antony, posted to Nairobi by a benevolent Shell Company, had just fallen victim to the current wave of pole fishing; his watch and wallet lifted at the Muthaiga Club during the night. Geraldine and Geoffrey, he was now on the staff of East Africa Command, were renting a bungalow in Nairobi with their two sons and a tame cheetah. When my parents arrived down from Ol Joro Orok the whole family was reunited in Africa for the first time since 1937.

With tarmac now extending even beyond Gilgil my parents' grey Humber Super Snipe reached their new house (named 'Oraimutia' after the little river) comparatively dust free. The large bungalow my father had planned, using stone and timber all cut on the farm, had a central stone section with a veranda facing their splendid view, which contained the spare room suite, a dining room and a little office. Projecting from one end of the central block would be my parents' bedroom wing and behind it the original kitchen quarters were connected to the dining room by a tin-roofed passage.

Put up in the guest cottage, a little cedar slab adjunct to the original property, I found both dining and bedroom portions already in place and a garden beginning to take shape. The next and trickier phase would be to dismantle the original wooden bungalow, which now projected from the other end of the central portion. Rebuilt in matching stone with a cedar shingle roof, it would provide their drawing room and a smaller sitting room, later to be known as the 'book room'. Fires were always needed at night, so two chimneys must be incorporated. The Italian POW who had served them both as foreman and master builder was about to be repatriated. Apart from Italian he spoke only Swahili, of which my mother had only the most basic 'kitchen' and my father at that stage none at all. My 'beautiful Swahili', as it was invariably known, was immediately in great demand.

I stayed almost a month, borrowing the farm's Ford 15 cwt and a houseboy (no-one, of course, travelled without a personal servant) to spend a nostalgic weekend with the Tryons. Sadly all good things come to an end. In Nairobi Geoffrey had pulled strings to get me an official air passage as far as Cairo and an invaluable 'interview at the War Office'. Even so I was stuck in Cairo for a week, where the Scotts again hospitably put me up. It was Christmas time, the height of the expatriates' social season. British goods consigned by visitors to avoid purchase tax were pouring into Egypt, where the British were now deeply unpopular. After several anti-British riots the government was about to appeal to the UN for the removal of British troops both from Egypt and the Sudan. David, slightly older than me, seemed unusually knowledgeable about current affairs, very busy with leader writing and book reviews for newspapers. Of course I had not the least notion he would end up as a Commonwealth ambassador with a GCMG.

Finally my not entirely spurious interview did the trick. A converted Lancaster bomber, returning from bringing the Emir Feisal home, took off around midnight and flew along the North

African coast. Half an hour from Malta we ran into a huge and dangerous thunderstorm. As the aircraft plunged and yawed in deep air pockets almost everyone, including the steward, began to throw up. It was like a scene from 'Vol de Nuit'. Several times the pilot circled drunkenly around Valetta airfield. Finally, swaying in with the wheels down, he realised at the last moment that he would overshoot and roared up again into the darkness. When we finally landed all of us had to be helped out, and in London several hours later I was still shaky.

Back in Berlin, where temperatures had begun falling to minus 40C at night, the Germans wore little black earmuffs, variously attached. A flatmate had kept the room where I lived in a well-to-do Grunewald mansion, and there were satisfying oohs and aahs about my 'adventurous trip'. Welcoming me back, the Chief Secretary said nothing about a grossly overstayed leave, only that the Foreign Ministers would soon be meeting in Moscow. There were several new faces in the secretariat and all hands would be needed at the pumps.

Hard at work preparing briefs, I heard I had failed the Foreign Service entry, as had a German speaker from the political division. I was disappointed, but not in the least surprised. One Sunday an exotic French-speaking American girl named Georgianna Pouzner invited about forty of us, mainly French and Americans, for brunch. We assembled in her flat at 11.00 am, ate scrambled eggs and talked our way through assorted food and drink until liqueurs at 3.00 pm. Soon afterwards she threw an even weirder *thé dansant*. I found the conversation at both these parties hard going, consoling myself after these tastes of the life cosmopolitan, "I don't think the Foreign Service was ever for me."

The staff of both the CCG and Military Government were now overwhelmingly civilian and some of the new intake had clearly come to Germany to enjoy a better standard of living than they could expect at home. But it was 1947, conqueror's rights in the past. In Berlin the authorities, struggling to curb the black market, suddenly introduced a system of official passes for the use of army petrol pumps. Not entitled to a car, I could only dump my Auto Union where the military police would find her, and walk away. Very inconvenient it was too! At Gilgil years before I had become good friends with a young district officer and his wife. It dawned on me that if I were to join the Colonial Service my previous experience should pretty well guarantee a posting back to East Africa.

After sailing through a preliminary interview while on leave that summer, I attended a final selection board at the Colonial Office. Questioned very searchingly about my readiness to serve anywhere in the empire, West Africa in particular, I gave some markedly negative replies.

Didi, her snow-white hair as luxuriant as ever in her mid-eighties, was still at Stratton Audley, but my Vauxhall had been sold. The Blackers, fed up with the additional wire erected in hunting country during wartime, had abandoned Bicester altogether and moved to the fens. Oxford was full of older-looking undergraduates – distinguishable from the locals, I noticed, by not wearing hats. There seemed really nothing to do. 'How I should hate to live always in England', I wrote in my diary. 'Neat little fields and tidy houses – so frustratingly civilised and well ordered'.

It was one thing to have failed an exam for an acknowledged pinnacle like the Foreign Service. Considerably stung by another less excusable rejection, I wrote at once from Berlin asking permission to appear before the Colonial Service selection board again. Meanwhile the army, similarly informed, abruptly posted me back to regimental duty. The Yorks and Lancs was a run-of-the-mill line regiment from the north of England, currently at Spandau and about to return to the Ruhr. Dire, I felt, on both counts. On top of this a wavy navy officer to whom I had paid a substantial advance to conjure me a new Chevrolet from the USA had disappeared with my money on demob.

'A' Company, which I was to take over, consisted of only fifteen men, who were preparing to instruct an intake of national servicemen due after Christmas. Arriving at Wuppertal in the Ruhr by train, the battalion moved into well-equipped barracks isolated on an icy hill top high above the long, narrow town, which had been shockingly bombed. Down the centre of the valley the Wupper ran under the famous *Schwebebahn* overhead railway. A new C.O., allegedly a martinet, joined from England, followed by his second-in-command and two more majors. About to lose my mini-command, I volunteered to become Education Officer and with it editor of the divisional and regimental magazines.

For amusement at Wuppertal there were occasional shoots for hares, duck, wild boar and deer in the woods. The battalion kept a few indifferent horses, which no one else wanted to ride. Enjoying some hacking, I gave up shooting for an ugly animal with a large head that must once have been trained for show jumping. In the exercise arena he cleared four feet easily, and could probably have gone higher if I had had the nerve or expertise.

Meanwhile our new Colonel lived up to his reputation. Pleasant enough to me, coming from another regiment, he was a stickler for

105

barracks efficiency, seeming to prefer the soldiers to his officers. In several of them he created a state of nervous anxiety which made for a nasty atmosphere in the mess. Work soon became a relief. With two instructors from the Army Education Corps I prepared a programme for two hours education weekly for 750 men. 'Dined with 1st Battalion Royal Welch Fusiliers', I wrote in my diary. 'A pleasant crowd with an excellent mess equipped with all their pre-war silver and fittings. This is a change from the Yorks and Lancs which our C.O. soon noticed. Otherwise all ordinary routine – a court martial, three Courts of Inquiry, several pep talks by the colonel, football matches, mess meetings – all as dull as possible. There is no field training and no sense of purpose. The troops are either regulars, often conceited about their dubious war prowess, or very young soldiers who are disinterested, idle and none too obedient. The war spirit is entirely lacking. I place my hopes on an appointment to the Colonial Service, or even rejoining the K.A.R.'

Delighted that the Colonel had allowed me to escape spurious junketing in the mess over Christmas, I went up to Berlin to spend Christmas with the Graham-Smiths. Alan was a former colleague in the secretariat. Their oven had been playing up and on Christmas morning Joan rushed into the flat's kitchen in more than her usual flurry. Failing to notice a German repairman with his head inside it, she slammed the open door on the poor man's ear and knocked him out cold. On Boxing Day I had a sore throat and felt mouldy. Two days later, with a temperature of 104 degrees, doctors at the casualty clearing station suspected laryngitis and began an ineffective course of M and B. At the General Hospital in Spandau they first thought typhoid. By now blurry with a very high temperature, I scarcely registered until tests finally revealed that my amoebiasis had returned, this time affecting the liver.

Back again on the familiar drugs, the Graham-Smiths came often to see me, leaving books. Nadine, private secretary to the head of the Political division had been my regular bridge and tennis partner. She had just returned from an inspection of the British zone by General Robertson, now Military Governor, and his wife in their special train. Arriving early one morning she had been called to speak to Lady Robertson. An honour guard of 11th Hussars was already drawn up along the platform, where her ladyship was waiting, after a bath, with her head poked out of the bathroom window. Unfortunately she had not realised that the train's glass was not properly frosted; behind it her ample frame loomed for all to see, stark naked. Of course we found this hilarious.

Determined now to leave the army, I was discharged from hospital early in February, feeling weak but well, and sent to England on a month's sick leave. From long discussions with my parents the previous autumn, I knew they would be happy to have me manage the farm they had perforce acquired on buying Oraimutia. My choices therefore seemed to be between the Colonial Service or farming in the Kenya highlands – 'a place', Elspeth Huxley had written, 'with a peculiar property of inspiring emotional affection.' This I too felt and had often seen in settler officers serving in the KAR.

In London the Colonial Office agreed to offer me another interview, but said it would be only for existing vacancies in West Africa. I have learned since that this was the common experience. Adding to my antipathy for the 'white man's grave' was the greater danger of reinfection by amoebic dysentery, for which no prophylactic existed. (That this was a genuine risk was surprisingly confirmed over four decades later in England, when an amoebic abscess suddenly developed on my liver.) Unsurprisingly I plumped enthusiastically for farming.

My friendly welcome back at Wuppertal was the more pleasant because in Medical Category 'C' I should not be staying. Rhine Army offered a staff job, but withdrew it on hearing I should be leaving the army. The Chief Secretary then asked me back to Berlin.

In terms of policy towards Germany the Allied Control Council had reached a parting of the ways. The Russians, actively dismantling and removing industrial equipment from their zone, still insisted that the Germans should pay reparations from current production, and not only from their own zone but from the Ruhr as well. In the west the British and American zones had been merged into one economic unit, we had eased up on dismantling equipment and instead were pumping in substantial subsidies to help the German economy back on its feet. Politically, free elections had already been held for German government at the Land (provincial) level.

A week after my arrival Marshal Sokolovsky walked out of a meeting of the Allied Control Council, of which he was currently chairman. Before the excitement had subsided the Russians announced they would be 'improving security' at their zonal borders. All military trains from the West, to Vienna as well as to Berlin, would henceforth be boarded at the zonal frontier and their contents inspected. We immediately cancelled our trains. On 5th April 1948 an accident occurred that sent the rising temperature soaring. A civilian Viking of British European Airways flying from

Hamburg to Berlin down one of the three agreed air corridors was buzzed by a Russian fighter. The two aircraft collided and everyone on board was killed. General Robertson immediately ordered fighter protection for all British aircraft, only cancelling it on getting a firm reassurance from the Marshal. The British press screamed blue murder.

A hundred odd miles from the British zone and surrounded by overwhelming numbers of the Red Army our situation looked precarious. In telegrams to London I noticed Robertson was advising against precipate or provocative action. Gradually the press furore died down. Then on 20th June, without Russian agreement, the three western powers announced the conversion of the currency in their zones at ten old marks for one new Deutsche Mark. The Russians reacted furiously. Closing their zonal boundary, they also stopped the barge traffic which carried thirty percent of Berlin's imports and exports. When we introduced the new Deutsche Mark into West Berlin as well the Russians withdrew from the Allied Kommandatura that governed the city. The breach was now complete. Ignoring our remaining all-too-vulnerable autobahn through Helmstedt, the western generals announced that all traffic to and from West Berlin would henceforth be by air.

O, ye of little faith! 'It is NOT clear', I wrote gloomily in my diary next day, 'how we and the Yanks will ever feed the western sectors by air alone. Will the Soviets let the Germans starve to get us out? Almost certainly, yes.' There was a lot even in my advantageous position I did not know. Robertson had not been Monty's brilliant Quartermaster for nothing: the necessary lengthening of our airstrip at Gatow had been completed the week before. Only a week later I was writing, 'Three hundred and fifty planes arrived in Berlin during the past twenty-four hours, a hundred and sixty of them British; Short Sunderland flying boats are landing on the Wannsee.' Between 26 June, 1948 and 30 September 1949, when the airlift ended, 2,322,738 tons of goods were landed at the three sector airfields, and life for the Berliners seemed to go on much as before.

Three months after the start of the airlift I flew down to Bad Oeynhausen en route for retirement. As one aircraft landed on the runway another was taking off. On full pay until the end of 1948, I was not quite due for the £1,000 that came with ten years' service and much too impatient to wait for it. Happily a similar sum for a 10% medical disability paid all my fares and later for a new car.

At the Thatched House my mother was on her customary annual visit, Didi depressed and disapproving. Having suffered from heart trouble in South Africa forty years earlier she had been warned not to go to high altitudes. Now, left alone in a sizeable house, the last of her grandchildren was about to follow her daughter into the Kenya Highlands, where she could not even visit. Sensibly saying little to me, she complained to my mother that it was quite wrong to have encouraged me, a waste of my training and prospects in the army. I would never have listened. There was an agricultural college in Kenya where I could get all the training I needed under local conditions. What more could I want?

i Our childhood home at Caulcott, Oxfordshire.

ii Ready for the Bicester Show on Galloping Gus, 1930.

iii *'Granny' Gertrude, my father, me, Antony & Geraldine at Berchtesgaden, 1937.*

iv *Self with Lieutenant-Colonel Euler, Private McCallum & our German staff car, 1945.*

v *Self, 1947.*

vi *Antony marries Mollie Northcote in*
    Nairobi Cathedral - her daughter,
    Judy, is in front.

vii *The original house at Oraimutia ...*

viii *The house as it became. The wing at left replaced the*
      original. The guest cottage is visible, behind right.

ix *(From left)*
My parents, me & Jane, Jill Downes, who married Archie Birkmyre,
Sir Henry & Lady Birkmyre. The bridesmaids are Birkmyre cousins.

x   Picking pyrethrum. Here the pickers lack the usual string bags hung from their necks.

xi   Cutting back dried-off pyrethrum in Kenya's 'winter', or dry season, at Kichaka.

xii *Our movable milking bails on Tuckerland, looking east. The cream
separator and milk tank are at the left with Samuel's recording table.
Water on Olbolossat can just be seen (right)
in the far distance.*

xiv *With Jane, Muthaiga Club,
c 1956.*

xiii *The wood burning pyrethrum
drier at Oraimutia, floored
with bamboo poles.*

xv The replacement of Van Dyk's burned-out building at Kichaka. Cost £3,000.

*xvi The river bridge over the Oraimutia is swept away again, 1961. Our
Citröen, my father & a visitor are on the farm side.*

xvii Kipkoske & my better polo pony, Georgia, with Susan on Black Beauty.

xviii Geraldine, Tim, Jill, David & Geoffrey Barton at the coast, c 1960.

*xix Building the labour camp at Kichaka, a task at which everyone
seemed competent.*

*xx   Susie & Rosie at Kichaka,
c 1960.*

*xxi   Unia & Co. at Ol Joro Orok, which
comprised also a garage, a railway
godown & a tiny butchery.*

*xxii   Berrow Hill House, Feckenham,
        bought & reluctantly sold.*

xxiii Settled at Finches, Pembury.

CHAPTER SEVEN

BY BACKGROUND and occupation my fellow passengers travelling first class on board SS Llandovery Castle, oldest and probably smallest of the Union Castle line, must have been fairly representative of the time. Sharing a cabin with me were a middle-aged official of the Kenya government and an agreeable misogynist going back to his lonely farm in the wilds of western Uganda. Some freeholds had apparently been granted near Fort Portal before 1916. Mrs Budgin and her daughter, Jane, were returning to their farm near Nyeri. Mrs Campbell with two small boys was rejoining her husband and Lieutenant-General Sir Arthur Dowler (with wife and two unmarried daughters) going out to Kenya as the new C-in-C. Mr Ramnell, Conservator of Forests, was returning from leave. Brigadier and Mrs Hurndell, retiring, as many did, from India, were going to farm near the Budgins and amusing Padre Geoffrey Lister, ex-Irish Guards, was on his way to the West Nile district of Uganda as a missionary. On shore I teamed up mostly with Bobbie and Pamela Sperling, a childless couple about ten years older than me, travelling on textile business, who intended finally to cattle-farm in Southern Rhodesia.

After calling at Genoa we spent two hours ashore at Port Said, where my diary records 'the touts resent being told to *'imshi'* (go way) now, although just as persistent themselves'. At Port Sudan it was very hot, 'an orderly little town, no touting. Spent a pleasant day in and out of the pool at the Red Sea Hotel'. Aden again 'some shopping in the bazaar. Crowded with Arabs, Somalis, Indians, the atmosphere thoroughly vicious. Bathed in a phosphorescent sea until midnight'.

The Llandovery Castle took twenty-four days to reach Mombasa, so there was plenty of time for reading. Alternating with 'War and Peace', I sat on deck enthusiastically studying 'Humus and the Farmer' by a pioneer 'green', Friend Sykes, and in order to understand better the arguments about white settlement, reading some of the recent history of this part of Africa.

Until 1900 East Africa had been administered from Zanzibar. When the gifted Sir Charles Eliot took over as HM Commissioner, he would shift his headquarters from Mombasa to a cluster of sheds, tents and railway stores on the plains below the Kikuyu escarpment, which would soon become Nairobi. Ten years earlier an agreement with the Germans had left Britain with a protectorate over Uganda. In addition to our long-time international obligation to root out the remnants of slavery, Uganda was important to us strategically. Whoever controlled the source of the Nile at Jinja controlled Egypt, and ultimately the safety of our trade routes through the Suez Canal. As everything going to or from Uganda had to be carried for hundreds of miles on a porter's head, the costs of transport were prodigious. A robust decision was therefore taken to build a railway from Mombasa into the interior, notwithstanding that there was not the least prospect of it ever making a profit. 35,000 workers were imported from India. By the time Sir Charles arrived 5,500 feet above sea level at Nairobi the expensive line was already well on its way to Lake Victoria.

Every train of course made a large loss. The first problem the new Commissioner thus faced was how to reduce the drain on the Foreign Office budget. No revenue could be obtained from carrying local freight as there was none to carry. Eastern Africa was very empty; most of the local tribes were pastoralists, moving and grazing their herds irregularly over vast areas. For three hundred miles between Mombasa and Nairobi the country was arid, and when the Commissioner travelled west, further into the highlands, he found that the Rift Valley and the fertile Mau escarpment beyond were equally empty. 'At times' he wrote 'one may make a journey from Naivasha to Fort Ternan (about a hundred miles) without seeing a single human, except the railway servants and their houses'. Elsewhere the native peoples did not grow even enough for themselves; famines were frequent and the concept of producing a surplus to sell was completely foreign to them.

The solution which Sir Charles Eliot urged on the Foreign Office, and was officially accepted, lay in white settlement. Settlers must be found to make the fertile land of the highlands productive. 'Beneficial occupation' was needed by a world still short of primary produce. Moreover some European civilisation would be an improvement, as the Commissioner saw it, on the 'blank, amorphous barbarism' of natives who walked around stark naked.

Sir Charles set up a Land Office and in 1903 enthusiastically backed a drive to attract settlers from South Africa. They would come, so the blurb said, to 'a climate of perpetual European summer' where 'ostriches could be had for the trouble of catching them' and there was 'a comparative absence of stock diseases'. The following year an influx of several hundred South Africans duly arrived, although a squabble over land registration – a precursor of the friction that continued to dog relations between settlers and officials – soon caused Sir Charles' resignation. In 1919, rather surprisingly, he became our ambassador to Japan.

The third Baron Delamere, who first arrived from Abyssinia as an explorer in 1896, shared with the erudite Sir Charles the belief that more contact with white civilisation would benefit the natives, and in 1902 he returned with his wife to live permanently in the territory. As joint instigator of white settlement and a pioneer in growing crops and raising stock under local conditions, Lord Delamere was to be the settlers' leader for the next thirty years.

By the time a further shipload of impoverished Boer families landed in 1907 the better land north-westwards as far as Nakuru in the Rift Valley had already been settled. With fifty heavily laden ox-wagons drawn by spans of sixteen oxen, and seventy-two horses, the Afrikaners trekked on under their legendary Kommandant, von Rensburg. From camp at Eldama Ravine the men of the party spent a week clearing a track up the Rift Valley escarpment through virgin cedar forest and dense bamboo. With their unique driving skills they somehow induced half-trained oxen to haul heavy loads in the rains up rough tracks and wet greasy hillsides to 9000 feet. From there they crossed an appalling area of swamps and reached a point that later became Eldoret, fifteen days drive from railhead. The grass on the empty Uasin Gishu plateau was long and teemed with game. For weeks they saw no sign of an African, their nearest neighbours, the Nandi, preferring to live in the hills. Shooting for the pot, they began to break and plant the veldt, and became in time the nucleus of a large Afrikaner community in Western Kenya.

More and richer settlers from Britain now began to arrive in the protectorate, which was already world famous for its big game. During the years immediately before the Great War maize, flax, sisal, barley, wheat and of course cattle were all being farmed more-or-less profitably at varying altitudes. Early in 1919 the Government launched its second official scheme to attract more settlers. 250 small farms of up to 160 acres each were to be donated free to ex-soldiers and around 800 larger properties made available for sale. The scheme was over-subscribed, and that November 1500 ex-soldiers and their families were embarked at government expense in the Garth Castle. Not all of the land they had been allocated was taken up, much of it in Western Kenya proving inadequately watered, but in the end ex-soldiers took up 1031 farms and the scheme was rated a success.

A book published in 1944, 'Race and politics in Kenya' (population at the time 17,000 Europeans, 40,000 Indians and 3,000,000 Africans), was then essential reading. In it the well-known, Kenya-bred historian and novelist, Elspeth Huxley, exchanged well-informed letters with Miss Margery Perham, Reader in Colonial Administration at Oxford. Discussing the fairness of many contentious issues, such as the amount of land reserved for use by Europeans, the level of wages paid to Africans or racial representation in the Legislative Council, the two ladies could agree only on one point: very little tribal land had been pinched from the Kikuyu for European settlement and they had already been amply compensated for it. As to the future, Elspeth Huxley argued for more self-government soon, and she thought Kenya would be 'a sounder and better country for the Africans and everyone else if the number of settlers were doubled or trebled'.

Margery Perham believed the vast majority of Africans and Indians wanted the Imperial Government to retain control. While both felt there must in future be more social equality and co-operation between the races, Miss Perham considered the part to be played by the settlers would be 'much smaller in scope and shorter in time.' In her opinion it would be twenty to twenty-five years (i.e. until the mid to late 1960's) before the backward Africans would be ready to begin 'a co-operative (which I presumed to mean with the Europeans and Indians) advance towards self-government'.

Much impressed by Margery Perham's command of detail, I was less sure about her conclusions. How could anyone look so far ahead or, doing so, have much idea how the empire would develop? India had indeed just become independent, but we had been there over two hundred years; Gandhi and his civil disobedience campaign had been around all my adult life. Africa was raw by comparison; here people talked of 'a hundred years' to do this or that. Above all it was the *British Government* which had first invited settlers to Kenya – and it was still doing so. A European Agricultural Settlement Board, set up two years earlier in 1946, had bought up the leases of farms whose owners had neglected them and had sub-divided large estates. Being under thirty-five, if I could produce £5000 capital (which I could not) the Board would take me on as tenant of a mixed farm of around 1200 acres. After some training at the Egerton College of Agriculture, the Settlement Board would lend me money at 4.5% interest for permanent buildings, installing water and fencing; once established I could buy the tenancy. Why was the government doing this? Surely only because the Kenya Highlands were uniquely suitable as a place for Europeans to make permanent homes. I discussed the book later with my father, who stoutly maintained that Elspeth Huxley had won the argument hands down.

My father was away when I reached Ol Joro Orok, or went away soon afterwards. I was on my own, gossiping with my mother, when a message came that a Mrs Wall was at the dairy. My father, it seemed, had reported that our heifers were failing to get into calf by the pedigree Ayrshire bull her husband had recently sold us. She wanted to test him. My mother always professed total ignorance of farming – as she had done previously of military matters – and at the time this was certainly genuine. While I could speak Swahili fairly well, most of my life had been lived in towns.

Rintari, the stock headman, was already at the dairy, an open-sided timber shed isolated on a long slope of wiry grass, as a herdsman arrived leading a young Ayrshire bull by the ring in its nose. We introduced ourselves to Mrs Wall. A brisk, middle-aged lady of rather military appearance in breeches and riding boots, she had evidently been kept waiting. 'Have you any cows on heat?' she demanded immediately. I looked helplessly at Rintari, who as usual understood more English than he let on.

'*Ndio*, Memsahib'.

'I'll need a sample'.

My mother and I watched as she unpacked a stout tubular object, carefully greasing the open end of its rubber sleeve, and eyed one another dubiously. Two dairy workers appeared, chivvying a crossbred Zebu cow, and after a struggle yoked her into one of the four stalls. The bull was already sniffing eagerly. He reared up. A long fleshy pink dagger shot out and Mrs Wall, tube in hand, stepped smartly forward. There was a scuffle. I stared fixedly at the cow's head as a warm glow mounted from my neck to my cheeks. At all costs I would not look at my mother.

"That should do", said Mrs Wall as the bull was led away. "I'll let you know in a day or two whether the semen is active." (It was). As I mumbled further apologies for the delay my mother emerged quietly from behind the dairy. "Not with you there, darling" she assured me as Mrs Wall drove away; and we giggled about it on the way back to the house.

Viewed from the main road at the exact point where, six years earlier, my armoured car had bogged down for the night, the trees surrounding my parents' snowcemed house stood at the right edge of their 567 acre property. Further to the right was a big expanse of virgin forest. Leftwards a large, bleak ridge of grey-brown high altitude grass inclined gradually upwards to a small patch of dense cedar forest at almost 8500 feet and the opposite boundary. A little arable planted on the saddle of the ridge fortunately could not be seen from the road: most of the pyrethrum there was 'blind'. Apart from a palm-thatched grain store alongside the access road, some corrugated iron sheets over the compulsory cattle dip and, somewhere in sight, about twenty head of low grade cattle, there was not a sign of development.

Of course it was not for the potential of this unpropitious hillside that my father had bought Oraimutia. He had simply fallen in love with the view. As the first rays of sunlight cleared the tall cypress hedge below my parents' garden, a rumpled duvet of white mist overlaying the great Olbolossat plain below would begin to tear and shred. Patches of water glistened among distant reeds. Beyond the plain, and across the whole thirty miles of their horizon, a sheer escarpment rose to the forests and peaks of the Aberdare range, so named sixty-five years earlier by the explorer,

Joseph Thomson. Silhouetted in the far distance, almost ninety miles to the east, were the symmetrical, snow-capped peaks of Mount Kenya. The colours of this magical panorama changed by season from fawn to greyish-green to near viridian, and during the rains storm clouds chased violet shadows along the escarpment.

During the past two years the house at Oraimutia had been transformed; a picturesque but primitive homestead had become a small but comfortable country house. Every bit of stone and timber, apart from cedar parquet flooring for the drawing room and cedar shingles for the roof, had been quarried or cut on the farm. Electric light had been installed via a Lister generator. Down in the riverbed a hydraulic ram (the nearest thing to perpetual motion ever invented) now pushed water through inch and a half pipes up 300 feet to a tank behind the house. What my father had not done much about was the land, bought at a cost of around £3 an acre.

Farming was to prove a most enjoyable occupation, even though, like fishing, usually practised at the wrong time. Our predecessor had relied for whatever cash the farm produced on growing pyrethrum, an insecticide crop introduced into Kenya from Dalmatia in 1928. A small factory in Nairobi extracted the valuable pyrethrins from dried pyrethrum flowers sent in by farmers, using a process of steeping in petroleum solvents. However, with the war over, unlimited demand for every kind of insecticide for the Far East had vanished. Hit also by competition from the newly fashionable synthetic, DDT, and the sudden release of American stockpiles in 1947, the market for pyrethrum had evaporated and the price collapsed. Production, which had been 3,000 tons in 1939 and 7,400 in 1945, had fallen back to what in the current 1949 season would be only 1,500.

The thirties in Kenya had been a truly awful period for farmers. After the 1929 Wall Street crash primary produce prices collapsed worldwide, and settlers saw the value of their maize fall in stages from a reasonable 12/- a bag to 3/-, wheat from 19/- to 5/-, both far below their production costs. Coffee was down to £45 per ton and sisal fared even worse. The African farmer of course suffered too, but was spared the worst effects because he ate most of the maize he grew. Some Europeans experimented hopefully with new crops. At altitudes over 7,000 feet the pyrethrum acreage increased rapidly, much lower down a pineapple industry flourished briefly until the war. Then in 1931 a dour, 'wild west' type named American Johnson, originally from the Klondyke, discovered gold. Many indigent settlers followed his syndicate to Kakamega, some thirty miles inland from Lake Victoria. One hopeful prospector was my friend Roddy Meyler, then managing a farm near Kitale, completely broke and surviving like most of the young men mainly on credit from his local Indian duka (shop). He spent several years at the mine, eventually panning himself a substantial £1,000 into the bank. Those who struggled on with maize or wheat grew it as cheaply as possible, turning to fertilisers to maintain yields from increasingly impoverished soil.

When war came many settlers joined the white territorials, the Kenya Regiment. By 1942, with thousands of troops in the country, maize output had dropped to a third of the 1919 level and there was nearly a famine. Galvanised by the British War Cabinet, the government finally introduced an 'Increased Production of Crops' Ordinance, which put maize growing on an economic basis. In the European areas a system of local agricultural committees was established, based on the War Agricultural Committees in England,

and soon afterwards control of agriculture was transferred from civil servants to a prominent settler politician, Michael Blundell, with the post of Minister of Agriculture and Natural Resources. A Guaranteed Minimum Return (GMR) also became the recognised basis for allowing credit to farmers to finance cereal growing. It was still so in our time and, combined with improving world prices, helped almost to double the colony's wheat acreage.

During the first forty years of farming at 5,000 to 9,000 feet on the equator quite a few settlers had risked their all in pioneering new ventures. Only trial and error had established that cattle dying by the score on the volcanic soils of the Rift Valley were suffering from cobalt deficiency, or how the equatorial short day affected plants introduced from Europe and North America. After Lord Delamere's death in 1931 a memorial to him had been built at Njoro on land donated by Lord Egerton of Tatton. This farm school was now a college under the Ministry of Agriculture. The post-second world war wave of Settlement Board tenants could learn whatever was by then known about farming under local conditions.

Back, clutching my notes, after an all-too-brief course at the Egerton College, I settled comfortably into the little two-roomed cottage. Our pyrethrum was down to eight acres. The Heinz collection of low-grade animals my father had inherited produced just one small churn of cream to go twice weekly to Thomson's Falls for butter making – usually in the boot of the Humber Super Snipe. So what now? I could survive for a while on the manager's salary of £15 a month all found, only a quarter of what I had been earning in the army. I still had some savings, but at 29 what of the future? For my one-third share in the farm, £3,000 nominal capital, I had sacrificed a private allowance. My parents would be all right provided the farm was not a financial drain, but I needed a third of some actual *profits* – and in farming terms, quite soon.

A series of post-breakfast discussions in my father's little office produced the first of many softly-softly approaches to capital expenditure. Wheat had almost bankrupted Lord Delamere when he gambled on it before the First War; lecturers at Egerton had said that seven recognised forms of rust (by the time we left Kenya the figure was a hundred) were liable to attack wheats at high altitudes. Moreover any substantial acreage would require a crawler tractor and heavy equipment such as our Afrikaner neighbours used. As for relying on increased milk production, the kind of grazing we had available would quickly dry off any self-respecting dairy cow.

In the end we decided to continue to fence new paddocks, thereby improving the grazing. Fencing wire we could import reasonably cheaply from the family business, Charles Wade and Company, steel stockholders in Birmingham. Oats for silage should grow adequately even on newly broken land; barley could be a money-spinner on the existing arable, provided East African Breweries would accept it for malting. Given our negligible experience of cereals they probably would not – then we'd feed it to pigs. We might try just a little wheat, but pyrethrum still seemed likely, in the longer term, to be our best source of profit.

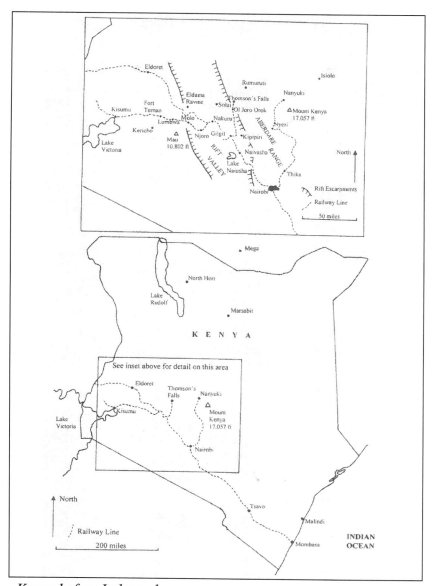

Kenya before Independence

To mechanise some of the planting and weeding, and to release the existing Fordson tractor from endless haulage work, we decided to buy one of the new little grey Fergusons, whose mobility and versatile implements with their three-point linkage had been demonstrated at Egerton. Finally we would stock up the farm with a bunch of low-grade yearling steers. They could be bought at auction for £5 a head compared with £30 for grade Ayrshires; hopefully they would fatten, even on our grazing.

At 6.40am each morning, as the sun cleared the Aberdare escarpment, my new personal servant Gichangi, a Kikuyu like the majority of the labour force, brought tea to the cottage. Beyond the suckering blackwood trees in a fenced paddock behind the house Maseno, the farm fundi, was finishing off the roof of my father's stable block. By seven a group of half a dozen barefoot young men in patched shorts and a rarely changed work shirt had assembled outside the big store, chatting until the headman called the roll.

'*Jambo*, Bwana Major' – an unfailing Kenyan grin.

'*Jambo wote.*'

Jembis, the long-handled mattock, might be issued for pyrethrum weeding, stone hammers for road mending. Someone had probably brought along a friend looking for work, who would offer his Kipande, the obligatory (and politically highly unpopular) work record. Starting wages for an ordinary labourer were about twelve shillings for a thirty-day work ticket, two pounds of posho (maize meal) and a bottle or more of skim milk daily, salt and sugar. Strung out in the sunshine down the access road, their piecework task might be to improve a stretch of road, unblock the log culverts, stone patch the deeper potholes. Now and then, half a mile away up on the main road, a huge red dust cloud would burgeon behind a lorry, then drift by, obscuring our splendid view. Working hours could be short. As I returned from the milking soon after nine for breakfast, the quickest worker would already be ambling towards his hut in the labour camp.

Itinerant contractors like the stonemasons, now busy in the little quarry above our top forest cutting out 9" x 6" stone blocks for the new piggeries, came and went, bedding in the labour camp and paid per running foot. Our real virtuosi were three contract pitsawyers, one of whom could write, figures anyway. Turning up with only sharp pangas, two jembis, a sledge hammer and a pencil stub between them, they would be issued with axes and a six-foot pitsaw blade, handled at each end. Together in the upper forest we would pick out a suitable standing cedar; fallen trees being seldom useable except for fencing posts.

A week later I would ride up on the new pony I used for Sunday polo at Thomson's Falls. The cedar would be lying there, neatly felled, its huge trunk now cut into fifteen or twenty foot lengths. Between them the men would have dug a pit six feet deep and manoeuvred the vast trunk length across it – don't ask me how. One atop (usually singing) and one in the pit, pulling in succession, they had sawn off four bark-covered off-cuts, which we used for the walling of huts and stores. With only the training picked up on other European farms they had marked the trunk core into baulks of 8" x 8" or 6" x 4" timber, then sawn out these baulks most accurately. The Ferguson's saw bench would later reduce them to the building sizes we needed. Magic.

Most weeks now I would be summoned to examine yet another dejected steer, head drooping, coat staring, temperature usually sub-normal. "What's the matter with him?" "*Hapana kula,*

Bwana", not eating. It had to be a symptom of something – but of what? When the first animal died my Egerton notes had been useless; Rintari suggested constipation, so we drenched the next with castor oil. It too died. We had not reckoned on vet's bills. John Andersen, our excellent Danish vet in Thomson's Falls, had to cover a huge district, so when he reached our next casualty it was only to do the post-mortem. Gall sickness, they told us eventually from Nairobi, not uncommon in cattle moved to new grazing at high altitude. Slow to plunge in with the trocar, we had already lost two cows during the April rains from bloat. Now, elbow deep at the smelliest end, I was learning that there could be no substitute for hands on, or more often in, experience.

Bumps and Timothy Walker, who farmed on the other side of the main road, were friends and the only neighbours we initially saw much of. Timothy, a large warm lady of middle age much given to hyperbole, preferred Ol Joro Orok to the dryness of their Thika coffee estate and, like my mother, was an enthusiastic gardener. Going round the developing garden at Oraimutia she showered superlatives until my mother's blue-flowered *Felicia pappae* became permanently known as *F. Timotheus Superba*. They were old settlers. Bumps once told me during the sudden coffee price explosion of the fifties that for thirty years their coffee estate had usually brought in £1,000 a year. Now he was paying £14,000 a year in income tax.

Even nearer to us, in a shanty on the hillside between the Oraimutia and the main road, a Boer farmer was shacked up with two Kipsigis wives and assorted coloured children. I am not sure we ever spoke. Miscegenation was rare in those days, producing half concealed smirks from our labour force when they drove past.

Van Dyk, an Afrikaner with eight hundred acres and steadily diminishing wheat crops, farmed on the hillside above our top boundary. We knew him mainly from his extreme reluctance to settle bills. Almost weekly the lanky khaki-clad figure of the post clerk from Ol Joro Orok, wearing a pillbox hat, could be seen on the hill opposite, leaning hard on the pedals to deliver yet another summons. We saw even less of the English neighbours up behind us. After a classic dispute about maintenance of the access road one of them had dug a ditch across his boundary to stop the other getting out. Who was in the right I have no idea, but after that only one oxcart came through.

Indispensable to our economy were the trek oxen with a skilled driver. When not pulling the wood-wheeled ox cart our patient pair of Zebus were always dragging something – a tree trunk for the pyrethrum drier, firewood for the Dover stove, a stranded car, even sometimes in the rains, a bellied tractor. On arrival of the telephone we no longer had to send messages by pony. It was a party line for, I think, ten houses. Our ring was three long, two short – and of course one could ring one's neighbours, or listen in, for free. This proved too much for one well-known gossip and her eavesdropping became notorious. Finally someone on the party line rang a friend. There was the usual click and sounds of heavy breathing; calmly he went on to tell a particularly filthy story. "Good Lord, where did you hear that one?" the friend asked. "Oh, Pam L...... told me." "I did NOT!" the lady exploded.

Inspired by a recent visit to South Africa, my father and Maseno created the final touch for my parents' new home. Emerging from its template, a white painted concrete shape, attractively curved in the Dutch style but without a lintel, was carried one morning to the front lawn and hauled carefully into position against the hipped roof of my parents' bedroom wing. Two days later a second gable graced the other wing, and finally a third stood over the central portion. The house was now complete. My mother, at more than sixty, had not managed the transition from sidesaddle to riding astride, so in the mornings she would garden while my father rode. None of us took to the local form of hunting: chasing duiker over farming land devoid of any fences except wire seemed pointless as well as cruel. Around the end of March the desiccating daytime wind would ease, grey clouds mass each afternoon on the south-eastern horizon. If our first storm broke before 5th April we said the short rains were 'early', after 12th 'late'. A month later my parents would take off for two or three months in England.

Early in the fifties my father returned with an enduring new enthusiasm. While in England he had attended a course for practitioners of the newly popular art of dressage, run by the then leading dressage guru, Mrs V.D.S. Williams. Much impressed by what expert obedience training could do to a horse, and now with plenty of time on his hands, he resolved to re-school his country-bred gelding, Inverclyde, from scratch. Throughout that winter, with the young syce he was training, he was out in the paddock beyond the blackwood trees, patiently lunging the horse on a long rein. As Inverclyde's suppleness improved, so did his head carriage, the rein got shorter. After that my father would mount for his morning ride.

More often than not there were visitors in their house. If they could afford the flight (and most of my parents' friends could), who would not swap staff problems and food shortages in a post-war

128

English winter for some weeks of Kenya sun? The opportunity to go on entertaining their friends under pre-war conditions must have been my mother's principal quid pro quo in agreeing to leave England. From October until March, with the spare room seldom empty, they showed their visitors around the farm and the district – there were no game parks then – entertained for them, if possible played bridge. There were seven staff in all, four in, three out, excluding mine. After such a long flight our visitors rarely stayed less than a fortnight – and that sometimes caused a problem.

I remember the dismay when a rather rich and well-connected lady, whom my parents had known only slightly back in Bicester days, asked herself, on and off, for a solid month. Not very long after her arrival – unfortunately she did not play bridge – it became evident that everyone would benefit from a change of scene. My parents, like others wary of the high altitude, owned at the time a bungalow on the beach at Diani, then a small village thirty miles south of Mombasa. Built of whitewashed coral blocks with a wide veranda under a steep makuti roof, it was set romantically thirty yards from the shoreline and backed by coastal scrub. Between veranda and sea only a line of tall coconut palms grew in the pure white sand of a picture-postcard tropical beach. Their visitor said she would indeed love to see the coast, so my parents dropped her in Nairobi to travel down more comfortably by train.

Feeling the need to put on more of a show than was usual at the coast, my mother loaded the Humber for their 450 mile drive with table linen, family silver and glass, and an extra servant. In the candlelight at dinner on their first evening she thought the table looked very well. Above their heads a monkey scampered across the roof. "Isn't this *wonderful?*" their visitor gushed, looking around "Now I know what it is really like living in darkest Africa".

After an overnight storm on the coast my mother noticed their gardener-caretaker, a local tribesman, bent double under a rope, struggling to pull an extremely heavy palm trunk up the sand to the bungalow. What on earth was he doing? "The axe is there, Memsahib", he explained. Many such stories circulated about the worthy but backward native, and said as much about European attitudes as about the locals. On the farm our workers still seemed trusting and open. A fading photograph I have from this period shows a young Kikuyu milker posing on the lawn. Dressed up for an important family occasion in his full tribal regalia, he wears an apron-like *kikoi* (sarong) embellished with colobus skin epaulets and grins away under a feathered headdress. Five years later he would not have agreed, let alone asked, to be photographed so intimately.

By the start of 1951, my third year on the farm, we began to feel the economic tide might be flowing our way. For newer settlers like us farming was a very serious business, and both the standards and the scale of European farming had risen since the war. On the Olbolossat plain, where I had hunted jackal, buck then grazed on grassland that stretched untouched to the horizon. Now there were huge fields of corn, mostly wheat (although the Settlement Board abhorred the old monoculture), eucalyptus windbreaks and tracks, occasionally a farm building or a crawler tractor at work. In 20 miles you might not see a single wild animal. At Oraimutia our pyrethrum was showing a modest profit and prospects for the industry looked brighter. We had acquired an enormous, newly fashionable Landrace boar and 8 or 10 Large White sows. Proceeds from our livestock seemed finally to have reached break-even.

Whether baconers or butterfat sales actually made a profit depended on the column in the analysis book to which one allocated inextricably shared costs, such as gristing in the hammer mill or transport. Thanks to a rise in the beef price, even our remaining steers had paid their way. Overall we were in the black, just.

Immediately to the right of my parents' garden when viewed from the road lay an area of mainly forested land with potentially good Kikuyu grass grazing. Owned by a Mr Tucker, a businessman now retired and living in Thomson's Falls, his 353 acres marched with ours to the river, and on the farther side bordered even denser virgin forest. With no access to it except through us, when my father made him an offer Mr Tucker accepted. Most of Tuckerland, as we always called it, was pleasantly undulating, its forest soil fertile. Much of the grazing was at first infested by the rank-smelling Mexican marigold and prickly sodom apple; elsewhere tall cedars, and on one hilltop a big spreading olive, stood amongst the forest undergrowth. There were enough dead and fallen trunks to fuel our pyrethrum drier for years. Although much work needed to be done, it was a beautiful stretch of country, the part of the farm I loved best. And owning it finally made Oraimutia viable.

CHAPTER EIGHT

ANTONY HAD LONG since fallen for a very pretty war widow with long blond hair, and had married her in Nairobi while I was still in Germany. Mollie Northcote already had a daughter, Judy, and they had another, Annette, before Antony was posted as Shell's number two in Tanganyika. I stayed with them there in the expatriate community of Dar-es-Salaam. Geoffrey Barton had retired early from the army. After a somewhat longer course at the Egerton College, he and Geraldine had recently bought an Olbolossat plains farm only six miles from Oraimutia. They had two boys now, born during the war, and a very new baby, Jill.

Before leaving for England in 1952, where Didi was about to be ninety, my parents had been staying with an elderly couple named Swinburne-Ward, near Njoro. Colonel Swinburne-Ward was retired from one of the posher Indian cavalry regiments and had been renowned throughout the Indian army as a horseman. Now he usually played second fiddle to his garrulous and notably indiscreet wife, a lady widely known in Muthaiga Club circles as '2LO' from the wartime news programme, "This is 2LO, Nairobi calling". Over dinner my mother confided her (quite unnecessary) worries about 'poor Russell' – whom the Swinburne-Wards did not know – being lonely on the farm. It seemed their nice neighbours, the Campbells, had a niece coming out from England soon. "Jane Birkmyre" 2LO went on enthusiastically, "of course we knew the name: well known business people in Calcutta. Family made a huge fortune in something – tea, I expect. She'll be a tea princess! We must have Russell over for the weekend. I know," she announced, "we'll give a dance!'"

Private dances were rare in Kenya and I had been to only one since my parents' welcome-home party for Antony years before. An invitation duly arrived after my parents' departure, Gichangi pressed my dinner jacket and on a Friday afternoon off we went.

The partner to whom 2LO effusively introduced me before the pre-dance dinner seemed young, rather quiet, very feminine, and pretty. On her green evening dress was a glitter of rhinestone jewellery which I rated 'English' and rather sophisticated, not 'local'. By the time dancing started and we had broken the ice, she was the only pretty girl in the room. Next morning 2LO asked whether I would like Jane and the Campbells to come to lunch, which seemed a good idea. In daylight I found Aunt Evelyn Campbell's habitually vivid make-up rather disconcerting, but she was friendly and charming. Gavin had been a regular in the 60th Rifles. Now they milked decorative little Jerseys on a rather smaller, neater and warmer farm than ours, and they knew, or knew of, my parents. The outcome, of course, was an invitation to stay a weekend with the Campbells. Never has the path of true love been more smoothly paved.

At weekends I was soon in thrall, tacking the thirty miles down through the bamboo forest to the Rift Valley, and the same up the Mau beyond, like a yacht around a buoy. Sometimes we met at polo, once in Nairobi and I drove her home. Publicly there was

134

nowhere to linger except the Rift Valley Club in Nakuru, so we often just drove around. My four-year-old Citroen Light Fifteen being already unreliable, quite a few hours were spent not unpleasantly by the roadside, and about two months later, on a scrubby bank below the Campbell's house, I popped the question.

A delighted Evelyn rushed off to cable reassurances to Jane's parents, who had sent their shy daughter out to Kenya only for a change of scene. 2LO, genuinely kind-hearted, was ecstatic. If she enjoyed telling everyone she had personally organised the whole thing, it was only the truth; we remain always grateful. Jane came over to stay with Geraldine, saw the farm and inspected the little cottage into which we should soon have to squeeze. Then, still high on excitement, she flew home by BOAC to prepare for the wedding and face the onset of some very understandable qualms.

In one respect my future wife was lucky. The English Rose about to be transplanted into the soil of colonial Africa originated, unlike me, from genuine empire stock. When her paternal grandfather, Archibald Birkmyre, arrived in Calcutta in the late 1890s it was to join the family jute mill, already established up-river on the banks of the river Hooghli. He married, had two sons, made and lost a huge fortune. When he died of cancer in 1935 he left his elder son, Jane's father Henry, not much more than the baronetcy he had acquired along the way. On the maternal side Jane's grandfather had been in the Indian Medical Service and, as daughters of the Surgeon to the Viceroy, both her mother and Aunt Evelyn had grown up in Simla, enjoying the social life of the Raj.

The climate of Calcutta being thought unsuitable for children, at the tender age of six Jane was sent to boarding school in England. Hilda Gowing, the family's Norland nanny, looked after her in the holidays, walking the lanes from her grandparents' house in Hawkhurst and teaching her about the hedgerow plants and trees (something I wish had been done for me). When war came, she was ten and her brother, Archie, nearly seven years older and at Radley. The Birkmyres, like many other families, wanted their offspring at home. With Hilda in charge of a large group, a liner loaded with children sailed from Liverpool via Durban early in 1940. An enemy raider was loose in the Indian Ocean, so when the ship lost all radio contact for several days it must have been an agonising time for the parents.

Thereafter, until she was seventeen, Jane went to school in high healthy Darjeeling, spending only the 'cold weather' around Christmas with her parents in Calcutta. For nine months of each year she and Hilda lived together in the plain comfort of the old Windermere private hotel, now quite unchanged as we saw recently on television. Even when out riding a syce would be sent to run behind her pony, named somewhat inaptly, 'Wait for Me'! No wonder she and placid, adaptable Hilda Doyer were devoted, and they remained so throughout her long life.

A month after Jane my cheaper Viking aircraft of Airwork Services Ltd touched down at Blackbushe Airport near Camberley. Quieter than the old Dakotas, it still took two nightstops to reach England. Jane and her parents were there in the Rover to drive me to Mandeville Place, where my parents often took a flat while in London. Jane had already deposited an empty suitcase in a flat near Holy Trinity, Brompton to become 'a spinster of this parish'; the banns had been read, we would be married ten days hence.

September 23rd 1952. Didi, her legs now badly swollen from dropsy, has been helped into a raised stall at the extreme end of the long Holy Trinity aisle. On our way out we pause and smile. Tears are running down her cheeks. I have never seen her cry before. Her last grandchild – and this is the only one of their weddings she has been able to attend. Momentarily I wake to reality as our limousine is stopped in a traffic jam outside the Hyde Park Hotel. To my right two old ducks in a bus are pointing down at us excitedly. They smile and wave, others follow. We wave back. A royal moment. The reception is at 23 Knightsbridge, Searcy's place, where we go up for still more photographs. Deeply tanned, hair shiny black, I am told to look down at my bride. "Lecherous Turk" she says later when the print arrives.

"You don't remember who I am, now do you, dear?" An elderly lady has planted herself with an encouraging smile firmly in front of Jane. The queue on the stairs waits patiently. Near the fireplace in the centre of the long reception room I can see my father looking very cheerful: he warmly approves of Jane. 'Gran,' Jane's other grandmother, is about to introduce him to her dimunitive sister, Aunty Daisy Black. Over the cocktail party buzz I hear disconcertingly Scots brogues, Aunt Daisy's is even stronger. The Dowager, as the family call her, perhaps ironically, is wearing a pair of long French gloves and keeps calling my father 'Major-General', a military solecism. Looking around there are not many people in the room I know at all well, not even on our side – but it is fun!

Next morning in our room at the Cadogan Hotel we decided on the spur of the moment to call on Didi. My parents, anxious to get home after an expensive summer and their lease already terminated, were on their way back to Kenya. It had been extremely difficult, my mother told me, to find somewhere Didi could be properly looked after. Finally the taxi deposited us in front of a very ordinary looking yellow brick terraced house a good deal further down the Cromwell Road than I had expected. Inside, the bedsit in the downstairs front room looked cosy enough. Didi's usual pile of books from Harrods lending library were by the bed, a bowl of flowers in the window. She was absolutely delighted to see us, wanting to talk to Jane and hear our plans for the honeymoon.

It was the first time I had visited anyone so old or in failing health. I was dismayed by the change in Didi's surroundings, but she assured us she was quite comfortable, her landlady a marvel, wonderfully kind. Her only complaint, poor dear, was that after aeons of evolution human beings had not evolved a better way to go to the loo. Being young and a bit thick, I missed the point and found this comical. We stayed about an hour. "Sad, isn't it," I remember remarking to Jane as we went to the bus stop, "there is no family at all to go and see her now."

At ten some evenings later our hired Wolseley saloon – 1936 model, engine reconditioned – was hoisted aboard at Dover for the night crossing to Dunkirk. 'Touring on the Continent' was less fashionable than 'in the West Indies', but a new experience for both of us. Emerging into the rain next day from lunch in a Saint Quentin restaurant, we found our Wolseley had acquired a puncture. Immediately opposite was a most convenient garage. 1,700 trouble-free miles later, on returning to nearby Roye, exactly the same thing happened. Odd.

In Switzerland, grey and overcast, a second night's B and B at Brugge cost us £2.16s, a shade more than in France. We bought a nice pair of prints in Innsbruck, detoured into Bavaria round all three of mad King Ludwig's exuberant castles and returned, pretty exhausted, over a snow-covered pass from Mittenwald. Then came a moment we both remember with wry amusement. We were on a long day's drive, whether before or after Salzburg I forget. The passing scenery was varied and spectacular. Probably I had been talking, and then for a long while there was silence in the car. The Wolseley hummed along. Jane, very young, shy and not naturally chatty, looked placidly out of the window. After a while I began to find this irritating: surely it was *her* turn? "For heaven's sake," I burst out suddenly. "*Say* something!" It was not a romantic moment (or even polite) but perhaps it marked our first awkward shuffle towards a highly successful and companionate marriage.

By 1952 damaged landmarks like the Frauenkirche and the back of the Rathaus in Munich had been cleverly restored. Indeed in the once opulent Ludwigstrasse it was only by looking upwards one realised that the busy shops at ground level had been installed in temporary bungalows within the gaunt shells of burned out brickwork. The autobahn to Karlsruhe was a delight, often not another car in sight. Our old Wolseley played box and cox with the ubiquitous VW Beetles, pulling slowly past on the gradients but being passed again on the flat. At Strasbourg 10/- for a portion of pâté de fois gras seemed excessive, so we pushed on to Paris, which neither of us knew, staying at a modest hotel in the sixth arrondissement.

On our last night in Paris, looking for a really good but not expensive dinner, we had scoured all the local streets and only at nine p.m. came on a modest doorway with the sign, 'Le Chateigneur'. There was no menu outside. Up a steep, narrow staircase the smallish dining room looked disconcertingly well appointed, the clientele rather smart. Now feeling committed, we chose from the unpriced menu what looked likely to be the two cheapest dishes, hopefully a cheapish wine, and dined well. When the bill arrived it was for far more than I had in francs. Perversely (though this happened) the head waiter firmly refused to change a traveller's cheque. It was now about 11.30pm. Leaving Jane incommunicado at the table I hurried to our hotel. The cashier had gone home, not only from ours but, as I half-ran from one lamp-lit street to another, from three others as well. Back at the restaurant almost an hour later, and still without cash, I found my bride sitting forlornly at our table in the now almost empty dining room. She may well, as she claimed, have been the focus of innumerable pitying glances. But her vigil had finally softened the staff: the restaurant would now be pleased to cash my cheque. Next evening we caught the night boat home. Driving up from Dover docks Jane enquired whether we had any money left. "Oh yes", I replied cheerfully, "twenty pounds worth." Ouch.

My father-in-law, Sir Henry Birkmyre, had been allowed to install a small canvas and belting factory in part of the family jute mill while it was in receivership, and this had proved particularly lucrative during the war. In the shadow of India's independence in 1947, he and his partner sold up. Making a common mistake, the family had first bought a handsome but too large eighteenth century mansion, North Lodge, on the edge of Battle. Soon finding this unmanageable, they upsticked to Cooden Beach, a prosperous coastal village adjoining Bexhill. From untarred Maple Avenue a minor public road to the station led past the indispensable golf course – my father-in-law being a fine and dedicated golfer, formerly an Open Champion of India and Burma. Substantial, brick, turn-of-the-century, Seagrove's white framed windows looked out with little regard for symmetry on a large well-kept lawn. Beyond some big fir trees were glimpses of flat blue channel: in all there were about three acres. Florrie, their nice cook, lived in and dailies arrived during the morning.

Coming down the stairs, I was beckoned into the dining room with the sad news, my mother-in-law told me kindly, that Didi had succumbed to 'flu soon after we left, that she had died ten days before and been buried yesterday in Solihull. It was the first time a death really hit me. Visiting England many years later in her own extreme old age, my mother felt she had not done enough for Didi, that she should have stayed on in England that summer. My father had died four years earlier in Nairobi, and she was determined to return there and be buried with him. Sadly, when this happened her own children too would be far away in England.

We were to stay until after Christmas in the bosom of Jane's quite extensive family. The 'Dowager' lived in London and Granny Austen-Smith, still very much on the ball, came round for tea most days from her hotel in Bexhill. Great Aunt Evelyn and Uncle George Buss on the distaff side had retired from Kent fruit farming, living then in Folkestone, while Jane's paternal uncle, Archy, and most of the paternal relations seemed to be up in Scotland. When adventurous great-grandfather Henry Birkmyre had taken a shipload of machinery to establish a jute mill in Calcutta, he had left behind the family's prosperous Gourock Ropework Company on the Clyde west of Port Glasgow, which had supplied lines for the Comet Steamship around 1810 and was finally sold to British Ropes in the 1960s. Numerous cousins still lived in a Birkmyre enclave around the small town of Kilmacolm, south of Port Glasgow; my father-in-law, always a courteous and punctilious man, was keen we should make them an early visit.

Before we caught the sleeper north my father-in-law 'had a word'. How would I like to address my in-laws? Not, we agreed, by any variation on 'father/mother' since my own parents were very much alive. Jane already used their Christian or nicknames despite a very large age difference, but to my surprise my father-in-law thought plain 'Henry and Doris' would be disrespectful, particularly towards his wife. Instead he proposed I call them in business fashion by their initials, 'HB' or 'DB'. I shall do this henceforth for convenience in writing. Orally I found it almost impossible, not to mention absurd, but failed to say so. In consequence, despite DB's periodic protests, I was constrained forever after to communicate with this intimate couple – of whom I grew very fond – while addressing them anonymously. Eventually I got quite good at it.

Pioneer great-grandfather Henry Birkmyre had been dead since 1900. At Kilmacolm his elder son's widow was still alive, as well as her four children, four grandchildren and multiplying 'greats'. Everyone of course knew, or knew of, my 'wee Jane'. She had spent many summer holidays at Dalmunzie, her grandfather's extensive mansion with it's own nine-hole golf course in the glorious scenery of Glenshee. He had even built a private railway to retrieve stags from the hill. Now sold, it would soon become a hotel. I vaguely remember grey stone walls at the factory in Gourock, a long shadowy vista down the ropewalk. More lasting is the impression of an extended family of many cousins rooted for generations in the same surroundings – circumstances so different from my own.

We returned to Cooden to read totally bewildering news of

attacks on both blacks and whites in Kenya. The murder of Senior Kikuyu Chief Waruhui, protest meetings of settlers, and on 20th October 1952, the declaration of a State of Emergency, had all taken place in or near Nairobi. Now the headlines named someone I knew, and close to home. Severely injured, her husband slaughtered after their servants had let in a so-called Mau Mau gang, Dorothy Meiklejohn had driven herself twenty miles on bad roads, one hand almost severed by a panga cut, to our own Dr Lowi in Thomson's Falls. That she herself was also a doctor, respected and valued locally because she treated many Africans, was apparently the still more confusing reason they had been chosen for attack.

When Jomo Kenyatta returned to Kenya in 1946 after 17 years away in Europe, he had immediately become the dominant figure in African politics. The Kikuyu adored him. Soon, however, he fell out with the Governor, Sir Philip Mitchell, backed of course by the settlers, over the pace for constitutional change. As we later learned, there was a tradition amongst the Kikuyu of organising violence through secret oathing and witchcraft to achieve tribal revolutions. Whatever part Kenyatta himself may have played in it initially, by 1950 a large secret society called Mau Mau had been instigated by younger Kikuyu, which was committed to driving white farmers off their land. Only the Kikuyu tribe was involved in this revolt and only two of Kenya's provinces were affected. However, by the time it was over many thousands of Kikuyus who refused to submit to the society's indescribably disgusting oaths had been slaughtered. A large proportion of these were Christians.

Memories of the mayhem in India in 1947 were still painfully fresh. Reassured by letters from my parents that all was quiet at Ol

143

Joro Orok, my in-laws entertained us generously and on New Year's Day of 1953 the eleven painted trays evidently thought indispensable to life in Kenya and other presents were loaded with our luggage at Tilbury. A week later we were enjoying the sun, and a rather distant view of Gibraltar from the rail of a Union Castle liner. A Royal Naval pinnace came chugging across the bay. Swept off in VIP style by my former section head in Berlin, now on the Admiral's staff, we were driven to a high point on the Rock. From there, the spectacle of a great armada of ships of all kinds in the bay is something we have never forgotten.

Sharing our table in the dining saloon were the wife of an officer in my father's regiment, Bridget Coles, and her three little daughters. The children ranged in age from about two to seven and by some bizarre fluke had all been born on 8 December, sharing one birthday. Unless addressed the little girls were to be 'seen but not heard', the axiom for small children amongst grown-ups on which we had all been brought up. If we arrived later than they at table all three, including even tiny Mary-Rose, would slip down from their chairs and bob us a curtsey. In short, we thought them such paragons of upbringing as we must try eventually to emulate with our own.

Anne Marshall, the daughter of old family friends, had been looking after the farm in my absence. She had had no trouble. Word at the duka, or outside Tanner Tremaine's dusty but quite indispensable garage at the Ol Joro Orok road junction, was that Mau Mau oathings were indeed taking place on other farms and labour was being intimidated. All, however, seemed to be happening on the farther side of Thomson's Falls. As caretaker, Anne's only innovation had been to promote Rintari from stock headman to *neopara*, or farm foreman; a shrewd move, for although barely literate, he was a natural leader. As a Meru from north-east of Mt Kenya, a tribe close cousins to the Kikuyu, Rintari could also speak the home tongue of the local majority without (we hoped) being so susceptible to the Kikuyu's internecine pressures. Samuel, a pleasant, and much better educated but unambitious Maragoli from Western Kenya, had replaced him, and both stayed with us until the end. We moved into the cottage, my normal work resumed.

"Where is everyone?" At roll call one Monday morning about six weeks later, only Kipsoi and Sawe, the two tractor drivers, and one other man were waiting by the big store, giggling together.

"They walked off yesterday afternoon." Rintari had trudged up from the labour lines.

"What – everyone?"

"Every Kikuyu in the camp – men, women and children?" I could hardly believe it. "Without their wages?"

"*Ndio*, just walked off. I've got all their tickets here, unfinished."

Had a gang entered the labour camp that Saturday night and frightened them into a sudden exodus? Or had our people been stealthily oathed over a period? We never knew. Among the remaining Kikuyus in the domestic staff, who probably did, it was a non-subject. Other tribes tended to shrug off Mau Mau activities as an aberration of the inconoclastic Kukes, who were thought too numerous and not greatly loved. Twenty or so men and women had simply vanished, presumably heading for their tribal reserve, and were not seen again.

If we had to lose three-quarters of our labour force, deep in the

145

dry weather with the dead stalks of pyrethrum already cut back was the best time to cope. Aside from two milkers, who could be replaced locally by Kipsigis or Luo, all the men who had scarpered without their earnings had been general workers. With a month to replace them before the rains began, our District Commissioner in Thomson's Falls recommended an immediate recruiting safari to the Maragoli reserve.

Jane moved for security into my parents' house and I took the Ford 15 cwt for the day's run to Kisumu. Leaving my hotel early next morning with a young Maragoli off the farm, we left the town and turned north-east, veering away from the shore of Lake Victoria. Once inside the native reserve a narrow earth road wound between tall stands of maize, varied sometimes by field peas or potatoes. Here every family owned and lived on its own shamba, which averaged about two fertile acres. There seemed to be no villages. Instead a vari-coloured patchwork of cultivation covered a vast, gently undulating and almost treeless plain, pimpled as far as one could see by clusters of thatched rondavels.

Calling to me to stop, my guide disappeared through a nearby fence, no doubt going home. Re-appearing with 'ndugu yangu' (literally 'my brother', but anything from a cousin to a friend) he said the chief wanted us to wait by a solitary fig tree about a mile up the track, which was evidently the local baraza, or meeting point. After an hour heads began to drift towards us around the maize crops and through the fences of the hinterland. When we had accumulated eight suitable young men I told them about Oraimutia, what wages and conditions we offered. Everyone smiled and said "Mzuri sana, bwana", very good.

Like most settlers I was lamentably ignorant about life in the tribal reserves, certainly unaware that the Maragoli was the most densely populated reserve in the colony. (What must it be like now Kenya's population has exploded?) Nor did I know that we were offering about treble the average cash income of a Maragoli family. None of the married men wanted to bring his wife to work on the pyrethrum; saying engagingly it was "better to see my shamba first." Two-thirds of all males in the reserve would already have been away, working in the highlands or at the coast; mainly womenfolk cultivated at home. A few Maragoli later joined us with their wives as squatters, cultivating two acres and keeping some sheep, while receiving wages but not rations. Meanwhile we had enough workers to run the farm, and even to continue our slow expansion.

CHAPTER NINE

AT ONLY TWO or three places along the Oraimutia's steep, tree-lined ravine could cattle get down to water. Now and then we would buy in a few in-calf heifers from Dick and Audrey Minns, a charming couple who farmed on the lower, warmer game plains near Nanyuki, but when these higher grades reached Oraimutia they were often a sad disappointment. Our main trouble was the long distances the cattle had to walk. Leys – 'my weeds' as Jane rudely christened them – were both difficult to establish and expensive. When not watering, the milk herd spent far too much potential eating time lumbering from a fenced night paddock or distant grazing to the dairy for milking. And the dairy's surroundings became a morass when it rained.

I forget where we got the notion of movable milking bails. Down in Nakuru, a four stall milking parlour was welded from heavy piping. With corrugated iron for roof and sides, there was a compartment for Samuel and his recording table, another to house a new petrol-driven Fullwood milking machine and its engine. All painted green – decades later we saw something very similar in the Jura hills of eastern France – the contraption was towed by tractor each week to new grazing.

It worked brilliantly. Togui, our primitive but wholly reliable herdsman, whose affinity with his charges equalled any biblical shepherd's, slept at night in one of the standings. The herd lay where it had been grazing. Back to the permanent dairy went cream separated on the spot and any surplus skim for the pigs, out went water to sterilise the equipment and milk churns, and in bad weather, dry firewood. Routines evolved. Now the little wooden hutches of milk-fed heifer calves were lifted regularly on to cleaner, healthier land – their baby brothers we ate. Milk yields began to improve and the calves too were less liable to scour.

When no visitors were in the house my father now regulated his life, or as he would have put it 'maintained civilised standards', through the discipline of time-keeping. The servants were well aware that the Bwana General required breakfast served on the veranda at 8.15am, lunch at 1.00pm, a siesta (goodness knows where my parents had acquired this time-wasting habit) 2.00pm – 4.00pm, tea 4.30pm, bath drawn at 7.00pm, dinner at 8.00pm and to bed soon after 9.30pm. Punctually. Being then only in his mid-sixties, my father invariably woke up around two in the morning and had to spend a couple of hours reading in bed. On car journeys to Nairobi he would look at his watch as each landmark was passed, muttering to himself 'on time', or with some irritation, 'we're late'.

Unable to speak any Swahili, with no kitchen of her own and almost literally on her in-laws' doorstep, Jane was not at this stage always happy. Her daily indoctrination into pursuits favoured by the Smallwood family began soon after breakfast with a riding lesson from my father, followed at mid-day by a session learning bridge. My parents were kind and extremely well intentioned, but I spent far too much time up at their house. Moreover, my mother was prone to 'drop in' and we lunched with them daily. At that sacrosanct hour I would often be far away on the farm: Jane had to face the meal alone.

The new manager's house was to be built just below our cottage, overlooking Tuckerland and a pretty, park-like valley of shade trees and short Kikuyu grass. Soon cut stone and farm-sawn timber were on site, actual building would be done by contractors. Jane, heavily pregnant, departed before Christmas to wait her time and endure larger, more intimidating spiders in Nairobi. Three weeks late, finally galvanised by a bumpy truck ride with us in the game park, Rosemary made her appearance at the Princess Elizabeth hospital. Childbirth was often rather easier in Nairobi than England, the nurses said, because of its altitude.

On the farm my mother's experienced Kikuyu cook, rolling up weeks late after leave in his reserve, was diverted to cook for us. The customary wood-burning Dover stove was installed in a converted shed and we ate alone now in my father's little office. Maseno added a little lean-to room for Rosemary on the front of our cottage. Tensions eased. Gichangi, my cheerful always willing personal servant, so quick at draughts I had got tired of being routed, had seemed genuinely pleased by my new marital state. Now suddenly, almost overnight, he turned rancid, his expression sullen and mutinous. Of course we knew that almost every Mau Mau attack on Europeans was made with the collaboration, willing or not, of the victim's house staff. He had obviously been oathed. We parted company immediately and Jane took on the first of a series of non-Kikuyu houseboys.

Like most farmers of my age I had joined the Kenya Police Reserve and wore my .38 service revolver around the farm. Jane bought herself a small pistol; at dusk we locked the cottage doors. One had to think seriously about precautions. Supper in the new house, which like my parents' had an outside veranda, would have to be passed to us through a window. About once a week, usually at night, I would be called to a police rendezvous, invariably on the other side of Thomson's Falls. A few of us then searched native huts, or more often lay concealed, hoping around dawn to spot a Mau Mau gang on the move, or see someone leave a suspect labour camp. Night was not a nice time for one's spouse to be alone; Jane certainly did not enjoy it. However, these patrols rarely saw hide or hair of a Mau Mau, and this rather boring occupation became known in the household as 'sitting under a bush'.

Once re-housed with a suitable spare room, we were ready to receive long-term visitors. DB, arriving by Comet in October 1954, was accompanied for a short while by her old mother, who went on to stay with Evelyn Campbell. HB came to us, as he usually would, via a business trip to tea gardens in India. Both parents stayed, on and off, until early March.

Although house help as such was not a problem (DB always charmed the servants) our infrastructure did not always make for entirely gracious living. Earlier that year a prolonged deluge during the main rains had swept away the logs of the little Oraimutia river bridge. Jane, in the village with Rosemary at the time, spent the next twenty-four hours baby-food-and-nappy-less with our neighbours, the Corbetts, on the wrong side of a raging torrent. Darkening from fawn to chocolate after a storm, water raised by the hydraulic ram was supposed to trickle continuously into a pair of galvanised iron tanks behind the house, and from there into our taps and loos by gravity. However the ram had been built into a bank twenty feet below a waterfall and driftwood coming over in spate often plugged the drive pipe. Twenty four hours later, usually on a wet weekend evening when the farm was streaming with water and visitors in both houses were going to their baths, an anxious houseboy would report *'Hakuna maji,* bwana*'.* There is nothing like having no water for inconvenience.

Electric light, for which Jane and I still depended on my parents' 3 kw generator, was either on or off. Breakdowns aside, it was also a mild source of friction. At precisely ten p.m. by the kitchen clock, when my parents would be comfortably in their beds with candles lit, twelve-year-old Adrieno, slipping down from his wooden chair, would lock the door to their kitchen, pause momentarily at the generator house to tip the lever on their Lister diesel and scamper off to his hut. In our sitting room below, Jane and I would probably be engrossed in a book or listening to an LP. As the engine died and lights rapidly dimmed, we must pick our way across the darkening sitting room to fumble, revolver in hand, at the locked door. Outside, hopefully not already smoking, would be a pair of rather smelly oil lamps – our lot until morning.

Such hardships and occasional tiffs with my father notwithstanding, Jane now had Rosemary, her own small establishment and garden. Lunching with friends after Sunday polo on the vlei ground within Thomson's Falls racetrack, we usually stayed on in typical Kenya fashion to tea, and for a final drink. I loved the life – autonomous in a splendid climate. To own land, to make virgin soil produce crops, raise stock and show a profit was deeply satisfying. In optimistic moments I saw myself still the founder of a dynasty.

By 1955 all farm workers' huts had, by law, to be concentrated into fenced camps. Like most farmers, we employed non-Kikuyu night guards. Within the Kikuyu reserve north of Nairobi nearly a million peasants had been moved for security reasons into villages – a process which, coincidentally, encouraged the consolidation of their hopelessly fragmented land holdings. Deprived of easy targets among a brave, loyalist, often Christian opposition in the reserve, Mau Mau gangs began operating deeper in the European highlands. Their numbers were increased by former squatters from the government's forest reserves around Molo. For many years these squatters had been allowed to cultivate large acreages of government land in return for clearing it and planting trees. When forced into camps, many of them, having come to believe their holdings belonged to them, became embittered and joined the Mau Mau.

Whatever the Mau Mau's total strength – the official figures of those ultimately killed, wounded or captured was 8,655 - the disgusting nature of their oathing rites and atrocities (overwhelmingly against their fellow Kikuyu), in a country which had a large white community, so shocked an already over-stretched Britain that she felt obliged to send in 50,000 troops. At weekends a carload often came up from the British battalion camped not far away to have tea and lie around on the lawn. Their officers were usually pleased to be in Kenya, other ranks missed the familiar, more urban surroundings of streets and pubs. "Look at that!" Jane overheard one exclaim excitedly as they were driven past my father's croquet lawn, "must be for polo!" Pleased and relieved as we were to see them, we did not at all realise that, politically, this tremendous military effort was to signal the end of Britain's support for White settlement.

Charles Corbett's farm next to us housed one of the government's so-called rehabilitation centres for known Mau Mau. One morning a gang was spotted nearby. Quickly assembling at Charles' house, eight or ten of us locals, all in the KPR, formed a line and began, revolvers in hand, to beat across a bush-ridden pasture towards the nearby forest. After about ten minutes two quick bangs were followed by much excited shouting. When we reassembled, Heywood Tremaine from the garage, a cheerful, very competent Londoner (who hailed everyone as 'squire', an expression then bewilderingly new to me) was as white as a sheet. Fifteen yards ahead of him a man had popped up suddenly like a startled buck. For an instant the two stared at one another, no doubt equally frightened: instinctively Heywood pulled the trigger. Bemused now at actually shooting straight, he doubtless wished he had not, for the African did not have a gun. Under guard in a truck two more deeply bush-soiled creatures crouched with dreadlocks down to their shoulders; on the floor lay his hirsute, emaciated victim in a filthy shirt, very dead. Unsurprisingly in such a nasty war, I heard occasional rumours of more culpable excesses, but these happily were the only active Mau Mau I saw.

Oraimutia itself was raided once. Stealing up at night on the small paddock containing our younger pedigree bull, a gang chopped the hamstrings of his hind legs. A horrid sight. Sadly he had to be shot. After this I collected semen from the senior bull and began to use AI. Fearing incestuous relationships we also imported semen from the government AI station at Kabete. The herd must have improved. The only sufferer was Jane, who sometimes found the baby food in our paraffin fridge displaced by somewhat unseemly test tubes.

Every year we planted some trees, mainly Eucalyptus for windbreaks and future firewood; I remember the young branches of some *Pinus Insignis* sagging to the ground one year under a four-inch layer of locusts – the only serious swarm we ever suffered.

Seeing a commercial van entitled 'I-Tech Moling' recently, reminded me of the tall, stately, wrinkled and very Lo-Tech individual, stark naked save for a thinning grey blanket invariably worn around his neck, who would amble as the main rains began in measured strides up the access road. His work tools, some supple sticks bound with twine, protruded from a very small Dick Whittington bundle. Our African mole was a rat at least twice the size and much more damaging than the English variety. For five cents each, twenty for a shilling – severed tails always to be produced as visual evidence – our nameless fundi would insert his sticks in their runs and bait them with bits of potato. Right across the growing pyrethrum fields, plump little bodies soon dangled above the plants as from tiny gibbets. The job done he would saunter urbanely whence he came, only to return next rains.

In the mid-fifties Jane and I drove up to Kampala to stay with Antony, now Shell Manager in Uganda. The lush smallholdings of the bicycle riding, banana-eating Baganda looked prosperous compared with the empty grasslands of the Kenya highlands. Crossing a long causeway at the recently opened Owen Falls dam across the infant Nile as it left Lake Victoria, we drove for miles past tall stands of irrigated sugar owned by the Madhvani family.

The day before we were due to leave Kampala, we had been out with Mollie admiring their large avocado tree when Antony asked me into his office. Shell, he said, had recently completed a worldwide assessment of the political and economic prospects of all the countries where they traded. He could not show me the actual report because it was confidential, but he had read the section on Kenya carefully. His advice to me (it was, I think, the first and last he ever gave) was to get out of farming by 1960. I was totally flabbergasted. In less then five years? "And do what?" I remember saying, "the army won't take me back." "Like it or not", he replied, "big changes are going to come quickly." In less than five years? In Kenya, where Shell had only recently taken on its first African clerks? There was not the education – not like the West Coast – and what about all the government promises to the settlers, its encouragement to take up land? We could not just be written off. Driving home Jane and I discussed the situation. After all, Shell could be wrong. The farm was just beginning to pay – and what else could I do anyway?

That summer we went, as promised, on holiday to England – not on 'home leave', which was something we never said: Kenya was home. Through DB, Jane was invited 'on her marriage' to one of the new style afternoon garden parties on the lawn at Buckingham Palace, which had replaced formal presentations. Suddenly the heavens opened and morning-coated guests began to push, commuter-like into the tea tents. I still remember the reek of wet mackintosh. As suddenly, the weather cleared. To some overt pushing and craning, the Royals headed by the Queen emerged into the sunshine. Someone tapped me on the shoulder. It was Winston Churchill. He smiled as we made way for him to join the royal entourage.

Later Jane and I rented an over-furnished little flat, deep in dust and the elderly lady owner's face powder, which overlooked the Brompton Road. On every red velvet curtain, every scarlet cushion and available excrescence, she had hung a cluster of equally dust-laden purple tassels. But it was well placed. We stayed for a week, exploring the new fashion for coffee bars, and doing theatres.

A few native sheep grazing around the farm with a *mtoto* had always been useful scavengers behind the cattle or horses and our absconding Kikuyus had obligingly left us more. Their hairy fleeces were not worth shearing. Some grew long front hooves that curled up in front like Turkish slippers, so they shuffled and slapped along in dry weather like old men. Grading them up a little with a Corriedale ram, we had used their male progeny for the table. Only the shepherd child himself could actually catch one, lunging suddenly from the middle of the flock to grab a startled hind leg. After an instructive sheep day at the Egerton College, and spurred on by cold, wet weather producing bronchitis amongst the weaners in our over-draughty pigsties, we finally decided to farm sheep commercially. In the shade of the trees below our house Maseno copied some holding yards in timber and bamboo, making a sheep race to isolate individuals or divide the flock.

Hedging our bets with a dual-purpose flock, we bought grade Corriedale ewes for their fleeces, and from John Poulton, a pedigree breeder near Molo, a handsome black-faced Hampshire Down ram. Soon christened Gumboots, he became a sly and violent butter. The wether lambs of his progeny would be fattened for the Kenya Meat Commission, the ewes provide wool; we would worm and feed them, trim feet and ring-dock tails by the book. Sheared for a wool clip by contract in February, sheep would finally be taken seriously.

It was 1957 when David Begg of Gilgil encouraged the dozen of us who played polo more or less regularly at Thomson's Falls to enter a club team for the aptly named Mug's Mug, the most popular trophy at Nairobi's four-day annual tournament. Polo players are handicapped anywhere between -2 goals (a complete beginner) and +10 goals (the world's best player) over a notional match of eight chukkas. This particular competition was for teams with a maximum handicap of 6 goals playing 4 chukkas, and designed for the many impoverished, like me, who owned only two ponies.

Nairobi members played host to visiting competitors and Jane and I were booked to stay in Derek Erskine's rather eccentric new house. A tall, shrewd and highly original Old Etonian, then in his forties, Derek owned Nairobi's largest European grocery. In a semi-political discussion over dinner the first night our host, distinctly left wing for the time, asserted that there was *one* field in which Kenya Africans could knock spots off the Europeans. He had, it seemed, taken the surprising step of timing Africans with a stopwatch as they ran different distances. He went on enthusiastically to prophesy that a Kenyan team would soon be entered for the Olympics. We had a good laugh about this afterwards.

Astonishingly we won through in the competition, and instead of the usual plated replica or engraved spoon, each of us received a very elegant silver cup with crossed polo sticks, made in Germany. Looking at it sometimes reminds me of that satisfying click, the whoosh to a sudden gallop in what is the King of Games (as well as vice-versa).

On 1st September 1957 Susan was born at the Princess Elizabeth Hospital, quickly and relatively easily between lunch and tea. Husbands were not allowed to be present at births, but exceptionally, being a stock farmer, I was shown into the labour room immediately afterwards. That, for both of us I think, was quite sufficient. Back at the farm my father kept to himself his disappointment at a fourth Smallwood grand-daughter.

When Dedan Kimathi was shot dead in the Aberdare Forest, the Emergency was virtually at an end and farm labour became plentiful. Each morning before breakfast twenty to thirty bibis, still mainly Kikuyu, and assorted children would turn out to pick on piecework. Both hands deftly nip-nipping at the white flower heads, they move slowly up the rows, bent double, transferring a handful of flowers at a time into the traditional woven bags of coloured twine that hang vertically from their necks. Wicker baskets for the overflow, assorted toddlers and an occasional nursing mother are waiting at the row end.

It is a pretty sight, row upon row of white flowers stretching away in the morning sunshine. As they pick, the women yack-yack-yack unceasingly to those on either side. The older women are topless above part-cured leather skirts, the younger girls in cheap and shapeless Indian cotton dresses from Unia & Co at Ol Joro Orok. Criss-crossing behind the pickers, quiet and endlessly patient, a forty year old from Kakamega searches for any mature flowers they have overlooked. Sometimes from across the field comes a sudden mock-surprised squawk, followed immediately by gales of laughter. Delving into a bag in search of immatures he has contrived, by mistake on purpose, to jiggle a pendant tit.

Oraimutia was now employing about a hundred people. We grew a bit of barley, for malting if possible, otherwise for the pigs, had forty cows in milk and a useful new whole milk quota was collected daily in churns from the (hypothetical) farm gate. In June a labour-hungry hay baler, operated from the Fordson's take-off,

160

pushed out rectangular bales of oat hay. As a second line of defence there was ronpha grass, a clumpy, drought resistant import from South Africa, which the cattle grazed behind an electric fence. Sheep on the whole were little trouble.

Now chairman of Assam Consolidated Tea Estates, a plantation company subsidiary of quoted Yule, Catto, my father-in-law had taken the plunge and bought two local coffee estates. Neither was in the traditional coffee growing area north of Nairobi, since the coffee boom had pushed prices there too high. Peet Estates, down in the warm Solai Valley about twenty miles from Nakuru, was a conventional one-crop plantation; the other, Heath Estates in hilly, high rainfall country beyond the Rift Valley at Lumbwa, was as yet better known for its herd of Red Poll cattle. Together they provided a good business reason for HB to join his wife in Kenya each year after a visit to the Indian tea gardens.

Evelyn and Gavin Campbell, retiring from their Njoro farm, had fallen in love with the coast. From their comfortable villa on Silversands bay, just south of Malindi, one could wade out at low tide to the protecting coral reef and snorkel down its face in deep ocean water. In February we would tackle the long, hot, dusty, deeply corrugated drive from Nairobi with the children. ("How far? Oh, still miles and miles and miles and miles.") In the Tsavo area one often saw elephant; magically after sudden rain all the bush there would be mantled with white convolvulus. The children searched in coral pools for starfish and one hot, boring afternoon during the long siesta, Rosemary cut jagged chunks from her pretty fringe with Aunt Evelyn's nail scissors.

When Gran, the dowager, died in London, Jane's father passed on a little capital. It was not a great deal but it always gave her in personal expenditure a welcome feeling of independence. My father and Inverclyde – now sadly dead of colic – had reached their equestrian pinnacle back in 1953 by winning Champion Hack at the Nakuru show and Reserve Champion in Nairobi. By 1957 he was the colony's senior dressage judge and when at home enjoyed teaching the young horsemanship.

Field and Farm, a small, illustrated magazine in Nairobi, was now paying me to write a monthly Farmer's Diary. Roger Hawkins, the jovial owner of a farm managing agency, who had beaten me roundly for election to the Kenya Pyrethrum Board, had made amends by offering the job of Visiting Agent to a nearby pyrethrum farm. Slightly better off – Oraimutia too was becoming profitable – I was feeling in need of a change.

No less blinkered than us, and despite the Mau Mau, the European Settlement Board continued to offer undeveloped land and low interest loans to white tenant farmers. A tract had just become available in Laikipia, some forty miles to the north of Thomson's Falls and west of Rumuruti. It would be lyrically described later in Kuki Gallman's book, *I dreamed of Africa*. My father came with me to inspect it. We found only straight bush – leleshwa and acacias without a single track, building or pipe in evidence. The newly made road on which we had come petered out, we were told, a few miles ahead. There was water, the soil looked good enough for maize or wheat, perhaps even for barley, but there was not enough rainfall for pyrethrum. Above all it was remote, pioneering country and none of us, least of all Jane with two small children, was remotely a pioneer.

Jane too was getting rather tired of living on her in-laws' doorstep. Yet to go it alone without the Settlement Board's backing

I would need working capital. Colonel Heath, managing director of the coffee estates, was probably more politically aware than we were, and was now keen to leave Kenya to start an oyster farm in Cornwall. My father, HB's other local director, had slightly strained his heart. To replace them both and administer the elaborate reporting system required by London, HB had appointed Dalgetys of Nairobi as Secretaries, with a place on the local board. Although well aware I knew nothing about coffee growing, he wanted me on the board too. Provided with a company Peugeot diesel, I was to visit the estates monthly and report back to London.

HB also said, very generously, that if we would not come 'home' (from now on this became a periodic plea) he would help us financially to expand locally.

Only weeks later I learned at the duka that Van Dyk had disappeared. Completely broke, according to money-wise Mr Kalidas at Unia and Co., he was living under canvas down in warmer Laikipia – presumably still trying to grow wheat. At his farm, sure enough, the large stone building with its rusty red corrugated iron roof and a flowerbed in front, which doubled as farmhouse and grain store, was empty and deserted. High on another large grassy down, the main road to Nakuru curled uphill at the farm's left boundary; there was better land along the hilltop. In a valley around the bottom was a six-acre dam and at the right corner a small stream joined the Oraimutia. Fordable there by pony, it was no distance to our stone quarry and only ten minutes back to the houses.

Back at home we discussed the possibility of renting. Pyrethrum, which of course Van Dyk had not tried, could be established with plant splits we had to throw away at Oraimutia.

Since Oraimutia was becoming rather overstocked, the farm's fertility could be improved to mutual benefit by folding some sheep on it. There were no huts for a work force: like most cereal growing Afrikaners Van Dyk had employed the minimum of labour. However, his dam was fed from a sizeable patch of virgin forest, which would provide ample materials to build a labour camp.

My inexpensive lease, to which Van Dyk readily agreed was to run for six years, terminable on six months' notice by either party after three. HB offered to provide £4,000 as working capital. Farmer's fingers crossed, I reckoned Kichaka (as we soon named it, *'Ki'* being the diminutive and *'chaka'* Swahili for a wood or copse) should reach break-even in two years.

African politicians in the Legislative Council (Jomo Kenyatta was still in detention) who had been pressing for more African representation, now staged a walk out. Faced by a constitutional stalemate, Macmillan's newly appointed Colonial Secretary, Ian Macleod, took a radically different line from his predecessors. By this time, the possibility of a multi-racial government was being suggested by moderate settlers like Michael Blundell and his New Kenya Group, as well as the opening up of the White Highlands. However, Blundell would still expect a careful balancing of racial representation in the Legco with representatives elected separately by each of the three racial groups. As we were to find out, this was not how Macleod saw it. He called another constitutional conference to be held at Lancaster House in January 1960.

Even before our lease began on 1st January 1960, my new recruits had begun to scare the handsome troop of colobus monkeys up in Kichaka's forest by splitting fallen trunks and cutting poles for roofing of huts. Down in the tall reeds below the dam their womenfolk chopped durable material for thatching. I bought a second-hand Ferguson tractor and trailer and, satisfied with progress so far, we left for the coast to celebrate my fortieth birthday with the Campbells.

As we returned to Nairobi, the daunting terms to which Michael Blundell and a more reactionary Group Captain Briggs (who cut little ice) had been obliged to agree were published in the East African Standard. Except in primary elections, when Europeans, Asians and Africans would still vote for their representatives as before, all future elections were to be held on the dreaded common electoral roll. Africans would thus be guaranteed a permanent majority in the Legislative Council. It was a scary prospect. The unfortunate Blundell (whom we supported) got a rough passage from a majority of the settlers. However, optimistic as we were, full self government had not even been discussed in London, and with no educated middle class must still be at least ten years off – or so we thought. Meanwhile, news that Britain had abandoned her political support for the Europeans in Kenya rang through the politically conscious minority in the rest of Africa.

CHAPTER TEN

DRIVING ON our upcountry roads was an acquired skill. So we were not overly surprised that Easter when two locals competing in the new East African road rally beat the best from Europe. It must have been some strange residual vanity that induced my father to buy a Mark VII Jaguar. Comfortable only on the tarmac, the most expensive of his numerous ditchings and minor mishaps in her occurred on the notorious Nairobi-Mombasa road. Keen to avoid the huge dust clouds that seeped remorselessly into the Jaguar's interior from every passing car, my father rashly decided to drive the three hundred miles overnight. Unsurprisingly his heavy, low-slung saloon bellied miles from anywhere, at dead of night, across one of the many splash fords that carried off floodwater. Pulled out eventually by a passing lorry, he had to finish the journey with the car on a train.

More circumspect, we had, like most people, stuck to continental cars. An Auto Union two-stroke that replaced my bachelor Citroen was followed by a reliable VW Beetle. In 1960 Citroen was causing a stir with their innovative new ID19, which offered front wheel drive and an entirely new kind of hydraulic suspension. Best of all, her clearance could be instantly raised from five inches on tarmac up to nine for ruts or potholes. Bought duty free in Europe and landed in Nairobi, this elegant two-litre would cost only £800. We decided to plunge.

Jane's deafness from otosclerosis was steadily increasing and, having now reached the age of thirty, it was time for the ear operation in London that her parents had arranged.

By June, with some old arable reploughed and cleaned of couch, I had bought a small flock of sheep and Kichaka's first pyrethrum crop was in the ground. Derek, my father's new manager, was installed in the guest cottage and would look after both farms in our absence. Jane and the girls flew to London overnight. Though my slower Viscount had to land five times to refuel, she no longer required a night stop. Coming round after the operation to her right ear, Jane had lain in bed puzzling over new and inexplicable noises – much clumping and scraping in the corridor. Finally she realised that what she was hearing was the nurses' shoes on the linoleum. Her operation had been an immediate and, as it proved, permanent success.

Whether lying down by the roadside or pumping herself up rear end first like a camel, the modernistic lines of the Citroen we collected in London drew admiring glances. At 7.40am on a September morning we drove up the ramp of a Silver City car ferry at Lydd airport and by eight were driving away at Le Touquet. Our *'gutes, mittelklassiges'* hotel on the outskirts of Sirmione – and indeed the whole of northern Italy – swarmed now with increasingly affluent Germans. Stopping on a high twisting road through the Apennines, I took the traditional colour slide of 'my wife and my car' which, ten years later, would encourage my first attempt at painting. Florence, staying at the English-speaking Pensione Hermitage overlooking the Signoria, we found more congenial and the locals less rapacious than in Venice. Dumbfounded by the sights, Michelangelo's David and later the incomparable duomo at Pisa, we vowed, as everyone must, to come back to Tuscany.

Resting from all this culture on the beach at Alassio, I observed how smart the Italian womenfolk were in their short skirts, also the preponderance of cats over dogs. Everywhere pushy drivers were going peep-peep in innumerable baby Fiats. Italian meals at the time seemed to consist always of pasta with house-reared veal or baby beef – one rarely saw a farm animal. Afterwards there would be fruit, cheese or the inevitable crème caramel. Menus were monotonous compared with France. In Cannes, where we stayed a night, no one dressed up: French resorts were less touristy. From a rather sleazy hotel overlooking the Vieux Port in Marseilles, we reluctantly handed over the Citroen for shipment out to Kenya. A ramshackle DC4 of Tunisian Airways to Paris having proved less unsafe than it looked, a Super Constellation from Orly took us home. In all, airfares included, a memorable twenty-three day holiday had cost just £10 a day.

Back in Kenya we were confronted immediately by the choice between a rock or a hard place. Either we go to live in the bleak, unplastered, cement-floored habitation Van Dyk had walled off from his wheat store – a dire prospect - or we spend a sizeable chunk of our strictly limited capital to make it habitable. Regardless of the political prospects, this would be money down the drain. Meanwhile Derek, a bachelor, agreed to live up at Kichaka and look after it as caretaker.

Three weeks later we had still not arrived at any plan. Then, around midnight one Saturday night, a messenger arrived from

Derek. The house was on fire. I dressed rather slowly and drove over. "And how is your mother?" the insurance assessor asked Jane, getting out of his car. He was the same man from Gailey and Roberts who had called when Oraimutia's pyrethrum drier burned down and he had clearly been charmed by DB. Derek explained that he had returned very late for supper to find that his houseboy had stoked the kitchen stove, gone off to his hut and presumably fallen asleep. An over-sized log must have fallen out of the stove: both the kitchen and the house itself were well alight, and he had barely time to salvage his kit. The assessor looked briefly at the sea of collapsed corrugated iron, then turned to us with a smile. "A total loss, I think, don't you?"

During the next few days farm workers were able to stack many hundreds of feet of readily reusable building stone, most of which had been laid without mortar. Our landlord needed another house, so did we; times being politically difficult, Freddie Dumbleton, the Thomson's Falls builder, could start at once to build a replica of our present bungalow. This time we decided to project the central section into an E, thus allowing space behind for a spare bedroom and bathroom. Having the necessary furniture already, our £3,000 insurance money would readily cover the lot.

The new house went up fast and, early in the New Year, with our furniture piled on the back of two Ferguson trailers, we finally made the move. It was only a three-mile journey physically, but much more emotionally. At last we had our own separate establishment and I a farm to turn around.

Facing east, Kichaka too had a spectacular early morning view of Olbolossat and Mount Kenya. The garden boasted a low walled terrace immediately below the house and a bed of tall, blue agapanthus; Jane added more of roses and fuchsias. Rosie, who had outgrown Helga Pears' little nursery school at the agricultural experimental station, had a little further to go on the school run to Thomson's Falls; Tabithai, the ayah, was around to amuse Susie.

It was a happy, relaxed time. At weekends we would usually drive for twenty or thirty miles – nearer fifty to the Carnegies – to have lunch and tea with the Meylers, the Pockleys or the Winnington-Ingrams, all of whom farmed and had children the same ages as ours. Back at dusk there would be houseboys to unload the car, and of course '*chakula tayari*, Memsahib', supper ready. Susie doted on her pet rabbit; we had Pushkin, a glamorous sealpoint Siamese, and a nervy, eczema-ridden Jack Russell called Vicky, to whom for the children's sake we had rather mistakenly given a home. In the lean-to stable were Georgia and Jaunting Car and a very safe, dark bay pony called (needless to say) Black Beauty, which Rosie had inherited from Jill Barton. Having seen horses around all of her life she was blasé and seldom rode him.

The small patch of forest at Kichaka's highest point soon became my favourite. Often, as I walked, green parrots would circle overhead or the colobus with their long black and white coats swing away through the branches. In its shadowy centre a reliable spring fed the dam and a pipe ran water to our house tank by gravity. Forest being essential to the eco-climate, our first priority was to install one of the new driers now recommended by the Pyrethrum Board. In Van Dyk's old machinery barn metal flues were laid at the bottom of a stone tank the area of two billiard tables. With picked flowers spread out on a permanent metal grill, they were dried by heat exchanger from a petrol engine. It was as quick and much more economical than Oraimutia's old oast.

With two seasons' of pyrethrum in the ground, and sheep penned at night on the area next to be ploughed, it became obvious we should pick more than our new grower's sales quota – an eventuality my original plan had rather glossed over. A field of rather weedy pyrethrum beyond the main road was being left unpicked. At the duka they said its Afrikaaner owner had gone off to join Van Dyk, and it occurred to me that he too might be bankrupt. Calling on spec on the Official Receiver in Nairobi, we made a deal. In return for maintaining our neighbour's better pyrethrum and handing over ten percent of the gross receipts, we could supply dried flowers against his sales quota as well as our own. This almost doubled Kichaka's potential revenue. Later a rather unusual crop of brussel sprouts, hardened in a dry weather frost pocket below the dam – 'Russell's Brussels' as they were promptly christened – sold well in Nairobi and provided wages money during the dead season.

Once a month I took the company's Peugeot to visit the two coffee plantations. The coffee bushes grew very tall up at Lumbwa, and for all the wrong reasons. Shale in Heath Estates' often almost inaccessible valleys blunted the tractors' implements, wore out their tyres and made planting very expensive. Worse still, the high rainfall that helped the Red Polls to flourish and collect rosettes increased the valleys' humidity. Year after year much of the crop was lost to the dreaded coffee berry disease. Heath Estates would eventually be sold at a loss.

Locals hardly ever used a hotel (hotels were for tourists, still few in number) so a night in the Tea Hotel at Kericho was an enjoyable experience. On my way home I would call at Peet Estates in the lower, warmer, drier, red soil of the Solai valley. This was real coffee country, flat as the Côte d'Or. Mason, the manager there, knew his stuff – all the routines of spraying, chemical weeding and irrigation – and reported on them regularly to the Secretaries in Nairobi. The coffee itself was planted in large blocks, the estate consistently made money. Whatever Mason may have thought of the supererogatory arrival of the chairman's coffee-illiterate son-in-law, he was always warily polite and I enjoyed my visits. Peet Estates too was sold after Uhuru; Mason sought his fortune in Australia.

We all worried now about our futures. To prepare for the impending primary elections, Tom Mboya, a brilliant Kikuyu soon to be murdered, and Oginga Odinga, a Luo from around Lake Victoria, had been organising these two tribes, which together made up half the African population, into a new political party, the Kenya African National Union. KANU was campaigning for the immediate release of Kenyatta and the introduction of African majority rule. Opposing it in KADU, the 'democratic' union afraid of the Kikuyus' land hunger, were the Kalenjin and all the smaller Kenya tribes. Many settlers foresaw a return to tribal wars.

At the 'Royal' that year, Nairobi's agricultural show, everyone was talking about the Beatles. Roy Walensky, invited from Southern Rhodesia to address a large and overwhelmingly European audience, urged us settlers to stand on our rights. He was loudly applauded. Five years later the settlers of Southern Rhodesia (now Zimbabwe), far more numerous in relation to their African population than we in Kenya, would indeed react by a Unilateral Declaration of Independence. For us such white settler mililitancy never seemed a viable option. Amid all this uncertainty, most upcountry people blamed 'Nairobi' and its officials. Some were

Correction:
Tom Mboya was also a Luo.

173

already leaving the country, heading usually for South Africa, and land prices had collapsed.

My parents, reconnoitring a retreat to one of the warmer parts of Europe, had been to Spain and Portugal one year, the south of France and Tuscany the next. Lucca was the place they preferred, but like some Roman commander retiring in first century Portugal, my father eventually concluded that Kenya and her climate really could not be equalled. Our friends the Meylers, out to the north of Thomson's Falls, had endured a nasty incident when early one morning a shotgun was fired through their bedroom window. Offered in his fifties the management of an estate in Suffolk, Roddy put his excellent manager in charge. After nearly forty years, he and Sheila were among the first to leave.

By the start of 1962 Jomo Kenyatta was already Leader of the Opposition. After the general election he would become prime minister: anything could then happen. We ourselves pinned our hopes on Michael Blundell. Although the objective of his party – a spell of genuinely shared government – never looked like being realised, it seemed at the time a very reasonable aspiration. Other white politicians still trumpeted 'settler rights', but we no longer seemed to have any.

Advocating racial tolerance in fluent English, Tom Mboya had subdued a hostile white audience in Nakuru. The Thomson's Falls District Association (Europeans only) now asked for another knowledgeable African politician to address them and, as its current chairman, I arranged for the speaker to lunch with my parents afterwards. The name offered to us was Daniel arap ('son of') Moi. Perhaps this meant something to the servants? Or was it just the unique spectacle of an educated, English-speaking Kipsigis arriving by car to lunch with the Bwana General? Like most settlers, nobody in our family had even seen, let alone talked to a fully educated Kenyan before. The meeting itself was not memorable, nor our conversation over lunch. Throughout the meal my parents' two houseboys waiting at table kept exchanging covert glances, sometimes smug little smiles. I wonder what they make of him now? "Nice manners" was our ill-informed comment as the young man drove off, "but not bright enough to get far against all those Kukes."

By now a nominated, if clueless member of the provincial Land Board as well as local director of Roddy Meyler's Siron farm, I used to call in there on my way back from Land Board meetings at Nyeri. Like everyone else, however, we were very conscious that time was running out.

At this fraught juncture HB generously organised and paid for a family game safari to the Serengeti – something, living in the country, we had never done. From the acacias of the plain with splendid views of Kilimanjaro, we drove south into Tanganyika. Nothing in the way of wildlife (one herd of elephants having always looked to me much like another) has stirred me so much as our first look into the Ngorogoro crater. A great rim-encrusted pizza, its vast dun surface watered at one side by a reed-filled swamp, it was spotted into the far distance by the darker shapes of grazing herds – wildebeest, Tommy, zebra all in the greatest profusion. Every species of Africa seemed to be down there, predators and prey immured everlastingly in a private, natural world of animals without man. After Ngorogoro the famous 'Treetops' and its artificial salt lick seemed ... well, artificial.

Speculation about our future ended abruptly one Friday

morning with headlines in the East African Standard. The British Government was to finance the purchase of one million acres in the European highlands on which to settle Africans. Our district would be included in the first purchase.

The ensuing chorus of excitement held more of relief than sadness: at least our farms would be again worth something. Many said they would take the money and go south to Southern Rhodesia or South Africa. Others (since work in tourism was a notion yet to take hold) hoped to manage temporarily for farmers further west. A Scots couple announced, with great satisfaction, that they could now open a B and B on the coast near Skye. Alone of our Ol Joro Orok neighbours, the Ballards, a childless couple living up our access road, who had come to high altitude from their Shropshire farm on medical advice, opted to stay put. Years later we heard that, much cherished by their smallholder neighbours for the help they provided, they were doing rather well.

Our decision was fairly easy. Oraimutia and Kichaka would be taken over together. Almost forty-three and having come out to found a dynasty, I was not ready to settle for farm management. There seemed little alternative locally. Land was apparently going free up on the Brazilian Matto Grosso, but we knew we were no pioneers. There were also the children's educations to think of. At the end of an exceptionally bitter winter in Europe, having given notice to terminate the lease and handed over Kichaka to Derek, I flew back, ingenuous, to England to look for a job.

Colonial brown and wearing a seriously dated British warm, I was shown into an over-crowded, old-fashioned city office near the Bank tube station which the chairman of Assam Consolidated shared, to my considerable surprise, with three other men. It was 29th March 1963. Everything felt totally unreal. Travelling down afterwards with HB to Cooden, I remember staring blankly at row upon row of small brick houses that flanked the railway line in Lewisham. Shiny wet cars were moving slowly down a high street, crowds crossing at the lights. What on earth were they all doing, these masses of people who lived here, so busy with their affairs? And what affairs? How on earth was I suddenly to become a part of them?

Well supported socially in Kenya, and having been a regular rather than a wartime officer, I had always enjoyed a certain status. For fourteen years I had been effectively self-employed. Now suddenly, without the capital to farm, no paper qualifications or experience for anything else, I needed 'a job' – whatever exactly that meant. Seen from the farm, I had thought of Britain as predominately an industrial country. Industry seemed to be her 'thing', as agriculture had been Kenya's, a job in industry would therefore be a good move. It was said to pay well. Moreover it might (I had never been inside a factory) avoid what had seemed to us in Kenya the ultimate, risible fate – becoming a commuter to London. But I neither could nor would agree to sell anything.

On the basis of these somewhat inchoate ideas, HB and my brother-in-law, Archie Birkmyre, had already begun to ask around. In some respects the time was propitious. Britain was probably still the strongest economic power in Europe. During the fifties, virtually anything had been saleable. With so-called 'full employment' and the welfare state launched, many in the business world were feeling pretty smug. Dressed in a new suit and overcoat, sporting a quite superfluous bowler hat from Lock's, I must have looked a good deal more 'with it' than I was. Anyway, within a fortnight a friend of HB who was developing a new security service in De la Rue, the printers of stamps and currency, offered me a definite place – £1,500 a year to start.

Then fate took a hand. In the plush and reassuring surroundings of the Savoy I had already talked to a stockbroking client of Archie's. Big, friendly, middle-aged, Roger Hunt was a director of a large and very fast growing group in the food industry, the Ross Group of Grimsby, and had married Carl Ross' sister. Soon putting me at ease, he told me that one of his functions was to keep an eye on the group's poultry business, which bred broiler chickens for the big chains and traded as Sterling Poultry. "You probably know that the broiler industry has grown tremendously in recent years? We are always on the lookout for the right kind of management", he had said flatteringly. "So if you would care to come up to Lincolnshire, where we are based, I could speak to the board about getting you some training."

Having vaguely heard of the Ross Group, the prospect of a job in a big agricultural business sounded exciting; 'security' began to look like an army-based sideline. After an anxious wait Hunt met me again. The board had agreed I 'join them' (an expression new to me); he wanted me initially up at Woodhall Spa, where I could stay at the Golf Hotel. My salary to start would be £1,000 a year.

Heading north at the weekend in the MG1100 that had replaced the Citroen, I found a pile of poultry magazines awaiting me at reception. Next morning Hunt arrived, very cheerful, in his imposing new Bentley and brought more poultry magazines. Himself Lincolnshire born and bred, he introduced me to the manager of the nearby Woodhall egg hatchery and drove away.

Once again feeling totally disoriented – first Kenya, then London, now this – I found it difficult to take in what was happening.

In essence thousands of eggs laid by Stirling Poultry's hens at farms around the district were collected twice a week, sorted, washed and loaded into the hatchery's five 'setters'. Their combined capacity was 150,000 eggs a week. Seventy percent of the eggs would hatch three weeks later into day-old chicks which, when they got bigger, would be moved to one of the company's broiler units. Broilers did not concern the hatchery as they were under different management.

As the days passed I asked loads of questions and sometimes joined the cheerful, knowledgeable fieldsman on his rounds, giving advice to local poultry farmers. Though the hatchery was more factory than farm, in the still deeply conservative squirearchy of the Wolds all the staff had backgrounds on the land and everyone seemed perfectly friendly and ready to help me. Jane, who had flown to England later with the children, came up for a weekend; soon afterwards I moved into a cheaper hotel in the village. The physical work, sorting day-old chicks and such like, was no more arduous and a lot less messy than I had been used to with cattle. Now and then RH would pick me up for a luxurious jaunt in the Bentley. And after some weeks I must somehow have passed muster.

Rosie was by now happily boarding at Ancaster Gate, a girls' prep school in Bexhill run by the estimable Miss Huxley, sister of Aldous, and her efficient partner, Miss Mumford. Susie, living with her grandparents at Seagrove House, went rather unhappily to a local day school. Up in Lincolnshire Roger Hunt told me I should be working henceforth in the study of his house. He most kindly offered to lend us an empty red brick, three up and three down, on the edge of his property near Aswardby. Jane came up. We furnished Park House with some of our Kenya possessions, which had arrived via Hull at a Spilsby depository, bought kitchen and garden equipment. Feeling more settled now, it was agreed we return to Kenya during the summer holidays to wind up our affairs.

In Kenya, Kenyatta was now Prime Minister. It would be months yet before any farms were taken over, but our district was in a state of flux. Most people now seemed reconciled to emigrating, though one or two thought of staying on, perhaps in tourism. Valerie Kent, a family friend, had paved the way. Her couriered tours for game watching were a growth market, and she and John, with their entirely mythical partner, Mr Abercrombie, were well on the way to making a fortune. With few options for the over-fifties, Geoffrey and Geraldine were managing one of many abandoned farms up in the Trans Nzoia for the Department of Agriculture. Personally I felt pretty chuffed. It was nice, as people expatiated on their plans, to be already 'fixed up' – particularly as no one else seemed even to be trying for England and industry.

Oddly disassociated now, we breakfasted in the sunshine on my parents' veranda. When the farms were finally taken they intended to move to Nairobi, but my mother was sad. Antony, now in Turkey, was also to be posted soon to faraway England. Pyrethrum picking was in full swing and my father said Derek had coped well. When all was settled, and some allowance made for my pyrethrum planting, it seemed that Kichaka would have kept us and returned all of our stake money. Good enough, I thought, after only three years. We sold the ponies, found good homes for Pushkin and Vicky and I had a long, nostalgic chat with Rintari. Then, in an odd role reversal, all the old hands who would be staying on Oraimatia came to see us off. In a flurry of grins and handshakes and *'Kwa heri'*, we waved our way for the last time down the drive.

Pausing another week in very hot Rome, the holiday mood continued. At Park House the children came up to us for the summer holidays. Here in the Wolds people were at once very hospitable, seeming as in Kenya to welcome new faces. The children were soon going to parties and we were being invited out to meals. Next door the farmer's bitch produced her puppies: "Mummy, Mummy, they all came out in plastic bags!"

Having once done a domestic science course, Jane had some notion how to read a cookbook but absolutely no practical experience. At Ol Joro Orok buying meat had meant ordering 'the best' for ourselves and 'topside' (extremely cheap) for the cats; 'fish' was one variety from Lake Victoria. When shopping for food in Horncastle she found her total ignorance of the right names or cuts distinctly mortifying. House prices locally seemed, even to us, surprisingly low. An impressive five/six bedroomed mansion with several acres was going in the next village for £6,000. Kenya friends came to visit and we began to think, semi-seriously, about buying.

Roger Hunt's main function for Carl Ross was to act as the predatory group's business scout and during working hours he was seldom at home. Every morning I would walk up to his comfortable study overlooking the lawn and a large copper beech, where Rossie, his nice, considerate secretary, fed me whatever reading he had allocated. There were newspaper articles, company reports and management accounts, very occasionally board papers, dealing with poultry strains and egg production, the economics of broilers, costs at packing stations, nutrition, diseases. I have the notes still. Stirred by this unaccustomed exercise, the left side of my brain woke up and each morning began to ache.

When Rosie returned to board at Ancaster Gate we felt that Susie, just six, ought to stay with us. Nowhere except the little village school, which we barely considered, was close enough for her to go daily. Solemn and vulnerable in her first school uniform, we deposited the little mite at Roughton Hall, an elegant Queen Anne manor house all of twenty miles away, to weekly board.

I had been working hard acquiring background, but as time passed and nothing was said I grew impatient and anxious. What had Hunt in mind? When would he introduce me to Carl Ross, or at least to Alexander, the Group MD? Unaware that here in England social life and business life were on entirely different planes, we went to a cheerful family lunch one Sunday with the sales director of Sterling Poultry, Lord Edward Fitzroy, and I took this as another indication that all was going swimmingly. Sent to study at Head Office in Salisbury, an able, much younger man, whom Hunt had previously recruited, did give me an inkling of some boardroom rivalry; and on my return Hunt warned me that over-production of broilers was hitting the firm's profits.

Summoned two days later to the seaside hotel where the group board was meeting, I finally bumped into Alexander. He wasn't a Scot of course, these being the upper echelons of the food industry, but a fairly recent Jewish immigrant from somewhere in central Europe. Emerging from the loo he gave Hunt's protégé one, quick, vengeful glare and brushed past.

In the Bentley afterwards, Hunt told me the worst. He had tried hard but the Board would not countenance my appointment. "What did you have in mind?", I asked eventually. "Initially", he said, "I wanted you to manage a hatchery with a broiler outlet." It would have been an excellent, practical job. Goodness knows what I had geared myself to expect – something more airy-fairy and elevated. Now there would be no job at all. I was doubly shattered.

We packed up, putting our furniture back into store in Spilsby. Poor little Susie, alas, would have to sit out the term as a boarder. Our new acquaintances all commiserated, saying they hoped we could stay on in Lincolnshire. Nothing concrete, however, came up until dinner on our last evening, when a local industrial knight offered me a place on his sales force. Having only just been denied, as I thought, the fruits of a plum job, I took this (whatever his motives may actually have been) as an affront.

Back at Cooden, HB loyally inveighed against Roger Hunt. We ourselves rather blamed Alexander, relieving our feelings by blacklisting all Ross Group products. For months neither could be mentioned without a hiss. The Birkmyres' initial contacts were now exhausted. I had no more idea than before what knowledge or skills the numerous industrial jobs advertised in the press actually entailed. What, for example, did a 'Production Controller' actually do? Someone suggested I might go on a course. Hearing that a three-week residential course called 'General Management' would be starting soon at the Sundridge Park Management Centre in Bromley, I drove up to see the Principal. It would cost me £200. Mr Connolly would give me whatever help he could in finding a job afterwards. So I enrolled.

CHAPTER ELEVEN

NEARLY ALL my business-suited fellow students at Sundridge Park's elegant eighteenth century mansion overlooking its own golf course were professional middle-managers in their thirties. Sent on the course by manufacturing companies – the largest group, appropriately, from Mars – they were state educated and spoke in a variety of regional accents. None had been to a public school, commissioned in the army, lived long abroad or was old enough to have served in the war. They were the norm and I was a creature apart – and I certainly felt it.

One afternoon a few days into the course, news came over the wireless that President Kennedy had been assassinated. United in the shock horror of this event, I finally found myself talking with other students. One of them – perfectly disposed to be friendly – began telling me about his job. "So what does everyone *do* in England" I remember asking him, "when they get home after work?" "Oh, they work in the garden," he replied, "mow the lawn, perhaps wash the car." All new to me. Was this life in England?

Having no experience whatever in commerce or manufacturing, I found it difficult at times to associate the techniques being advocated with a real-life situation, but intellectually it was not unlike work at the staff college. Put next to me in class, and often into the same work syndicate, were two older cousins from family businesses, both with public school backgrounds. William Kenrick, the elder, was about twelve years older than me. He had been to Rugby and Oxford where, I was much impressed to hear, he had got a First in Classics. His family business in West Bromwich, of which he described himself deprecatingly as the gaffer, had started in the eighteenth century as iron founders of domestic hardware. After falling on very hard times, the company had recently been rejuvenated in the nick of time by taking up the patent of a new, diecast furniture castor, named after its, I think Australian inventor, the Shepherd castor. Even the big company people seemed to have heard of this castor's commercial success and soon Mr Connolly introduced a case study based on it. The younger Kenrick was a director of the larger, better known Kenrick printing company, also in West Bromwich.

Over the years the Kenrick family had evidently been big cheeses in the life of Birmingham. Both my parents too had hailed from that area. Soon I was expatiating to the older man in his rimless spectacles – and sometimes to both Kenricks together – on the pleasures of life in Kenya, and on my problems for the future. When the course ended Mr Connolly sent for me to say he had found no-one with a job to offer – whereas, to his evident surprise, I had.

Back at Cooden a letter soon arrived from William Kenrick, Chairman and Managing Director of Archibald Kenrick and Sons Ltd, appointing me his personal assistant at £3,000 per annum. This was a shade more than the average GP earned. HB seemed impressed. Unaware that in industry the salary offered conveys status, I simply thought Kenrick was being rather generous.

Mr first task, Kenrick had told me, would be to investigate and report on the market for Ironite. This small subsidiary product was sold from a separate sales office in London; it was against the grain, but I would have to commute. We took the monthly lease of Tanners, a solid three-bedroomed family house on the edge of Wadhurst in East Sussex, so named by a retiring grocer after the source of his capital. Snow returned in quantity that winter and there was often ice *inside* our windows. Susie went daily to Bricklehurst Manor, her school number three.

Pulled along by the claustrophobic rush hour crowd that surged through the ticket barriers each morning, I emerged flustered from Sloane Square tube station on my first day at work, and with some difficulty located the little Ironite office. Down in the basement of a house along Holbein Place Mr Douglas, a stocky, stiff, grizzled individual old enough to be my father, had his desk under the iron-barred window. Behind him in the whitewashed interior I was introduced to the other tenant, Geoffrey Greenall, a retired gunner officer of about my own age; the two of them shared the services of a part-time secretary. In an adjoining little room Greenall stored samples of his company's bottle storage cartons, together with a new sales item, 'Jiffy pots' for gardeners. There was a loo next door and a flight of steps led up to street level.

Seated opposite Douglas, I heard myself awkwardly putting those what? where? when? questions about Ironite I had culled from the Sundridge Park notes. Douglas' replies were as brief and defensive as possible. Ironite, I gathered, was sent up from the Kenrick works in West Bromwich. Used somehow in the surface of concrete floors, it had almost magical qualities – though I could not gather quite what. At mid-day Greenall, who loathed his job, took me for a pint at the Rose and Crown in Lower Sloane Street. I was not yet used to pubs, after living so long abroad, and bitter was something of a medicine. Over lunch, Greenall explained that the old man had been taken on by Kenrick after the war, straight from the Military Police. Never very bright, he was now a pensioner with an invalid wife at home and spent as little time there as possible. "Ever since William Kenrick told him you were coming," Greenall said, "the old boy has been in an absolute fever of apprehension. He's sure you are after his job." There were several perfectly respectable occupations about which, at the time, I harboured priggish reservations. Advertising, for example. But that anyone could actually *want* to be a salesman – and for Ironite – struck me as totally bizarre. Greenall, I dimly but rightly realised, already had me down for a fish out of water.

Some weeks passed before I finally felt driven by conscience to start asking architects, civil engineering contractors and builders' merchants about the saleability of Ironite, which was simply a concrete floor hardener. Driven occasionally to making calls blind, because no one would give me an appointment, I still have a vision of opening the door of factory offices somewhere in Middlesex. A meeting of middle managers was in progress. Older than anyone present, very bronzed and (being out of the West End) properly dressed in my Cork Street country suit, I started in officer accents to say I was looking for the Chief Engineer.

"Who do you represent?" someone asked eventually.

"I don't represent anybody," I remember exclaiming indignantly, "but .....". Buyers were generally kind, because I was so obviously suffering.

Soon it dawned upon me that Ironite was no more than swarf

collected, gristed and bagged off the foundry floor. It had helped Kenricks to weather a slump when it was priced at twelve times its production cost. Now it was at eight times, and a competitor in Manchester, which I also visited, had entered the market at five times; Douglas had a problem. All this I reported to the works, where they must of course have known about it already. After two miserable months a message came from William Kenrick saying his Board had decided to bring in management consultants at West Bromwich. He would like me up there as soon as we could find accommodation.

West Bromwich lying to the west of Birmingham, the countryside around Kidderminster looked suitable and at weekends throughout the summer term we made the five hundred mile return trip across country. A mile over the Severn at Bewdley, its tall end brick wall by the main road topped by a very elegant chimney, we soon found just the house we wanted. Queen Anne with a delightful garden and pond, Mill House was definitely a gent's res; if the price was a bit over our limit, it was not expensive for so much style. After a third Sunday visit – the owner was looking for somewhere to retire in Worcestershire – we decided to stay in Kidderminster overnight and return in the morning to put down our deposit. Next day the owner's wife opened the front door, led us along a corridor to the drawing room. As we chatted cordially over a coffee, from beyond the end wall came the rising growl of a lorry engine. Mounting to a roar as it passed, almost rattling the cups in their saucers, the noise dropped as the driver changed gear on the hilltop, altered pitch and droned away. A couple of minutes later came another, then another ... coal lorries, the lady explained, beginning their Monday morning run from the Black Country to the South Wales coalfields. The house was on their direct route.

Luckily for me, Mr John, the cousin who ran the London sales office, now fell ill. For a few weeks I found it not unpleasant to turn up in Newman Street and, guided by his efficient secretary, take a few telephone calls concerning castors or domestic hardware. At lunchtime I would wander across Oxford Street and Soho Square to eat in one of the Italian restaurants along Frith Street, most of them still quite affordable. Mr John's three southeast salesmen, all very flush from over-generous commission on sales of Shepherd castors, wafted me in their plush company cars around the ironmongers in their territories. But I was only an onlooker. A sales trip to Bexhill and Battle proved rather too close to home; as my 'colleague' took the proprietor's orders, I remember feigning an intense interest in the shop's stock.

Summoned to Birmingham by William Kenrick, he was waiting for me at the station in a long tweed overcoat and driving gloves, more like a family solicitor than my idea of a Birmingham businessman. We drove around in his comfortable family saloon, lunched, I think, at his house. He talked about the city and his connections with it, of which he was evidently proud, and of course I claimed my Smallwood connections had been quite influential too. After lunch, Kenrick explained that when I came up to the works I should be meeting his brother Hugh, the sales director, and Lunn, his long serving company secretary. Working alongside me with Dean, the resident management consultant, would be Martin, his youngest son, who had just completed a B.Com in Dublin and was coming into the business. Explanations completed, he took me back to the station.

Unfortunately any behavioural guidance William Kenrick may

or may not have been trying to impart on this solitary occasion simply did not penetrate. Floundering in a very strange new environment, I was also confused about my relationship with this older man, who was now also my employer. I had little idea what he was expecting *of* me, not sure either what he intended *for* me. And the latter, lamentably, was what intrigued me the more.

Not finding a house, we decided to rent for six months east of Droitwich in rural Worcestershire. Our landlord, a retired brigadier and his wife, glad to have congenial tenants, kindly saw us in with a house-warming party of their neighbours. Then Hugh Barham, who had daughters the ages of ours in nearby Himbleton village, turned out to be my father's cousin. As in Lincolnshire, our social life got off to a flying start.

The M5 motorway ended at this time just north of Droitwich. After pleasant open country and the drab, working class suburbs of Halesowen and Dudley, fifty minutes drive brought me to a characterless commercial road that culminated at its top in West Bromwich high street. Below the high street, and dominating its surroundings (most of which have now disappeared under the M5), was the great red brick rectangle of Archibald Kenrick and Sons, Ltd, each corner of a roughly four-acre premises surmounted by an angular, pinnacled tower in the apogee of Victorian gothic.

After parking in a bleak side street, one entered the high façade through a formal archway flanked by the works office and its workforce time clock. Inside the perimeter of buildings, a wide, rectangular cobbled alley circulated the works and gave access to more buildings in the centre. Directed to use the first door on the left, I found myself in what looked like a warehouse. Uncarpeted stairs at one corner led up to a stark wood-floored area some fifteen feet high and lined with linoleum, evidently in use as offices. Up again, I clumped across more bare boards the size of a badminton court to three glass-panelled, temporary offices in a corner. Two of these were slightly larger than the third. In the first William Kenrick himself came up to introduce me to Tony Dean, a pleasant dark-haired man in his mid-thirties, resident consultant for the PA Consulting Group, which also owned the Sundridge Park Management Centre. The next office to his would be mine. In the last and smaller one Martin Kenrick, a blond young man of around twenty-five, shook hands, I thought, a trifle warily.

At this time, of course, I knew no more about the workings of a factory than of a nuclear power plant. The Kenricks employed in total five to six hundred people, of whom perhaps fifty were office or sales staff. Unable to recruit iron foundry labour during the post-war boom, the family had introduced West Indians. Now, like other firms in the black trades, they found that, once thirty percent of any workshop consisted of coloured labour, it was difficult to retain white labour.

After a week or two of shuffling papers, Dean began to send Martin and me into the offices, ostensibly to collect him some information. Unlike Dean, I was not an outsider, nor like young Martin, family. Middle forties and talking in the accents of a Kenrick, everyone must have seen immediately that I was entirely ignorant of everyday clerical systems, like Kardex, or even what the different commercial departments were supposed to do. Worse still, I was no more at ease in talking with the Black Country staff of a long-standing family business than they with me. In the machine shop or foundry, where a muttered "How do you do" seemed disconcertingly to mean "Good morning", I clearly knew nothing about engineering either.

It soon became obvious, even to me, that all but the most routine of decisions were made in a big spartan room adjoining the sales department on the first floor, where William Kenrick had his desk by the windows with his amiable younger brother, Hugh, the Sales Director, opposite. Between the gaffer and the door sat his forty-something company secretary, Mr Lunn, who looked after the books, pay and employment. The engineering complexities of mass-producing Shepherd castors were handled by a Mr Donkin. The only non-family member of the three-man board, he was middle-aged, clearly a wizard at his job and rarely to be seen in the offices. I never spoke to him. Everything else requiring a decision came via a supervisor or foreman directly to the gaffer himself. Yet now I was in the works, Kenrick consistently ignored me – as a deeply suspicious Mr Lunn was clearly only too glad to do too.

In Kenya meanwhile, my father had decided, faute de mieux, that African self-government was going to be perfectly all right – a position from which he never thereafter deviated. During the property slump accompanying Kenya's independence, my parents had bought for a quarter of its previous value a large, comfortable villa on a sixteen acre plot at Karen, just outside Nairobi, and renamed it 'Kichaka'. My mother, nearing eighty, set out to improve the garden with a bougainvillaea walk. In England even their richer friends had by now been reduced to part-time staff, but the Oraimutia establishment had transferred lock, stock and barrel to Karen. England, as my father remarked when my parents came to see us that summer, was now a completely different world; but Kenyatta willing, as he proved to be, their pre-war life style could continue. Oraimutia had been taken over in 1964. My share of the proceeds was calculated at £6,000: not a lot to show for fifteen of the 'best', and certainly happiest, years of my life, but twice my original stake. Many had fared much worse.

From Himbleton we and the children enjoyed the hot, saline baths at Droitwich Spa, almost as buoyant as the Red Sea. Susie started that autumn at the Alice Ottley junior school in Worcester, school number four. As Christmas approached we had already looked at about thirty houses for sale. We were becoming anxious about the end of our lease when we heard of Berrow Hill House, a little further to the east near the village of Feckenham. A brick extension seemed to have been added early in the previous century to a much earlier cottage. There was a little courtyard, a length of lovely brick wall projecting into a convenient sized garden, and the property looked out across its own four acre field towards a stretch of unspoiled countryside.

Encouraged by the offer of an interest-free mortgage from Kenricks, we paid £11,000 (ten per cent too much) and engaged a very efficient firm of builders. The kitchen was completely renovated, central heating installed; for the first and only time we would have our own en-suite bathroom, and there were walk-in cupboards for my dressing room. Dust still everywhere, our furniture arrived from Spilsby and we were obliged to move in.

Jane, who had bought a second-hand Mini for the school runs, now scoured Berrow's Journal, Britain's oldest newspaper, for any mention of house sales. In the antique shops of Droitwich and Malvern Victorian furniture was still cheap, Edwardian not yet in fashion. Second-hand prices were often mouth-watering, and for a few hundred pounds she almost filled the new house:

Chesterfield and two upholstered armchairs   £10

| Pair of Victorian rosewood chairs | £8.15.0d |
| Edwardian inlaid table | £8.10.0d |

At work Dean recommended producing a smaller range of more standardised products and, more importantly, that the directors introduce a proper management structure. The board agreed. For the first time authority was to be devolved to qualified, non-family managers – a Sales Manager, Works Manager, a Chief Accountant and a Production Controller. Advertisements were placed in the national press. To my surprise, I was told to sit in on the preliminary selection interviews, which Dean would be holding in the PA Group's Knightsbridge offices; final selections were to be made by the board. Thus, silent and often mystified, I contrived to attend my very first formal job interviews on the employer's side of the table. I also saw, during those two days, the kind of experience and paper qualifications an interviewer looked for, and successful candidates usually had; most of their professional certificates I had never even heard of. Back in West Bromwich my presence at the table must have confirmed every suspicion of me.

In the high hedged, twisting lanes of Worcestershire we were finding people very friendly, and slowly we began to feel more settled. It had just penetrated my long Kenya orientation that mid-sixties England was not really the same country I had lived in twenty years earlier. Next to Berrow Hill House there was a mixed farm whose gruff and roughish owner, Mr Richardson, rented our four-acre field for grazing. Calling one day at his modest farmhouse with its somewhat dilapidated buildings, I found Mr Richardson out so asked for his son. "Oh, Tom," someone said, "he is away at University – learning agriculture." They were nice people and I was glad.... but a son getting to university from such a background? This was certainly different from the England of my school days.

A couple of months later Dean stopped coming in, his report finished, and I found myself lacking a function. Kenrick remained aloof. There was no kindred spirit in the offices and I had naively done nothing to cultivate young Martin. In the lunch hour I would buy sandwiches and wander disconsolately down grey West Brom high street, all small drab shop fronts and an occasional bleak industrial pub. The new managers began to arrive. Abruptly, and without a word from William Kenrick or any job description, I found myself posted on the notice board as Administration Manager. This (potentially authoritative) position had not been among Dean's original recommendations. Status without substance: I had no notion what I was supposed to do.

The outcome was of course inevitable. One Friday morning not long afterwards we heard that Kenrick had sacked his entire sales force. Summoned to the directors' office I was castigated for "wasting your time, not fitting in." Offering me a generous six months pay in compensation, Kenrick admitted that during the past year he too had 'learned a lot about the peculiar nature of commercial life'.

In retrospect I think this was a fiasco for which we were both responsible. With an army background, and absolutely no relevant experience socially or commercially, my manner went down badly in the works; I needed someone to tell me how to behave, and also what to do. As for William Kenrick himself, he was not really a business manager at all, but had landed in his position by inheritance. From this, and the endowment of a good brain, he had acquired a sizeable chunk of arrogance. Of course neither of us would have got any marks at all as a communicator.

Contemporary opinion on the whole sorry affair was perhaps best expressed by the most mature of the new entry, the sales manager from Bowaters. "William Kenrick should never have done it" he pronounced, "but having done it, he should have made sure it worked."

CHAPTER TWELVE

WHATEVER WILLIAM KENRICK may have gleaned from this experience, I was still at the bottom of my learning curve. It was nice at first to be at home. The Pockleys, like us somewhat adrift, were farming from a bleak stone house deep in Pembrokeshire. We visited them, people came to us, mostly family. Still set on a job in industry, six quite pleasant months passed and I had achieved only one job interview.

My constant prop was a stalwart neighbour, Richard Bagnall, a director of Tube Investments, who now advised trying for a job in London. To repay the Kenrick mortgage we put the house on the market. Although British industry was grossly over-manned and unproductive, the unions at the time constantly bayed for ever-larger pay increases. As our estate agent from Cheltenham played two or three potential buyers for the £15,000 we needed, Harold Wilson (who had already devalued the pound, though not 'in our pockets') demanded six months of 'severe restraint' on incomes. All but one of the interested parties promptly withdrew and the following week the housing market collapsed. Yet somehow avuncular Mr Chamberlain still got us our asking price and returned to me all my Kenya capital. At the end of the 80's the local couple who bought Berrow Hill House sold it for £350,000.

From the Birkmyres' new and smaller house built in the grounds of former Seagrove, Jane went into hospital for a hysterectomy. Susie joined her sister at Ancaster Gate, Bexhill, school number five. My father would pay her school fees – still in the low hundreds per term – as HB was already doing for Rosie.

I will draw a veil over the next few months; homeless now as well as jobless, we parked on my unfortunate in-laws, then rented for the holidays. My initiative stuttered to a total stop, somehow spontaneously rekindled. It was Mr Connolly who finally revealed what two labour exchanges, where I had drawn the dole, had both failed to tell me. There was an employment agency in London, the Officers' Resettlement Bureau, which was ready to handle, not only retiring Service officers, but also anyone who had once held a commission. Immediately I found that the interviewers in its warren of rooms spoke my language. And, for the first time in all my job hunting, I could see others of my ilk in the same boat. That too helped.

From the bureau's basement in Belgrave Square I went for my second interview to the Engineering Employers' Federation in Broadway House, a large, comfortably carpeted building opposite St James' Park tube station. The EEF (not an oily rag in sight) represented the country's largest industry and negotiated periodically with the unions nationally to fix wage rates and working conditions in engineering. Another particularly busy function, I was told, was the handling at national level of official (as opposed to wildcat) industrial disputes, which had not been resolved in one of the EEF's thirty-odd regional associations. Offered £1,600 a year – still twice what a qualified nurse then earned – as an extra hand, I was invited gently to read myself in.

We rented a flat in Earl's Court for my probation, leased a small house in Sevenoaks, again for six months, from another but less cordial brigadier. Rosie, now thirteen, moved on to Ancaster House School, where Susie rather regrettably followed her later. Houses around Sevenoaks proving expensive, Jane spotted one, privately advertised, further south at Pembury. The lady owner wanted £10,250: we settled down at Finches.

For the next eighteen months I was concerned mainly with correspondence and the industrial courts that then met national union officials at York monthly to discuss (and occasionally resolve) disputes within the agreed procedure. In 1968 a long awaited report of a Royal Commission concluded that periodic collective bargaining to fix the pay rates and working conditions for a whole industry was nonsensical. Instead, pay levels ought to be negotiated between managers and shop stewards at the plant or company level, then set down in agreements which took account of a firm's commercial situation. This process they named 'productivity bargaining', which became instantly the 'in' buzzword.

Seizing on productivity bargaining for its now statutory prices and incomes policy, the Government legislated that any collective agreement to increase employees' pay must also provide for an improvement in that firm's productivity. But how exactly was 'productivity' to be assessed? Some guidelines were laid down, but this was way beyond the training of an Employers' Association's industrial relations staff. The government set up a large advisory unit to help other industries, and the EEF, representing the largest, decided to base some advisers of its own at Broadway House. An advisory service director and a team leader were recruited from the

PE Consulting group, volunteers invited. Keen now for more than pen pushing, I volunteered and was sent off for basic, mainly work-study, training in management consultancy, followed by numerous courses.

Supplied with a car and housed in Dartmouth Street next door, four of us (it soon became three) began two-day surveys of the many, usually smallish federated engineering firms around Britain which were facing pay demands and in difficulty because of the productivity clauses. Sol, our clever team leader, was an experienced, professional management consultant. Ian, with whom I usually paired, had formerly been a production engineer in the aircraft industry, then MD of a small company making buses. None of us – and rarely anyone we met – was a qualified accountant.

Very aware now, after Kenricks, that simply writing more of our reports, as I did, would not justify my place, I started trying to master the productivity angle. Someone on a course must have mentioned Added Value, a much less familiar concept then than it is now. Gradually I realised that changes in the company's payroll costs in relation to its value added could be used to satisfy the productivity guidelines. Later I cudgelled my brains (a bit of pride comes in here) and wrote a manual on Added Value, which was published by the EEF for its associations. In the employment boat I had found at least the semblance of a paddle.

Nearly seven years after we left Kenya Jane and I took the girls to visit my parents at Karen. At West Bromwich William Kenrick was soon to be killed in a road accident, Martin would rule in his stead with Lunn esconced on the board. Before we returned to England Rintari came down to see us at Karen, bringing with him Thuku, our old cook. As ex-headman Rintari now owned fifty acres of Oraimutia. Still living in his old hut by the cattle dip, and farming exactly as we had shown the way, he was making a fair living. Thuku, with only the usual ten acres and several wives, understandably grumbled about having to spend half the year away cooking for tourist safaris.

Yet Rintari too seemed to have much to complain about. Already, he said, there was far too much corruption at Thomson's Falls: KANU people pulled the strings, while *karanis* (literally, the clerks) got all the better jobs and the perks went to former Mau Mau. Travelling around, friends had told us something of their own problems since Kenya became independent. "Be honest", I remember saying to Rintari after an hour or so of chat, "would you really rather have me and the other *Wazungu* (Europeans) back again?"

Rintari thought for a moment. "No" he said firmly, "things are better as they are now." And this, with a job and a bit of know-how finally under our belts, was how we had come to feel in England too.